Wetlands of the Northeast: Results of the National Wetlands Inventory

April 2010

Ralph W. Tiner

Regional Wetland Coordinator

Northeast Region

U.S. Fish and Wildlife Service

300 Westgate Center Drive

Hadley, Massachusetts 01035

This document should be cited as: Tiner, Ralph W. 2010. Wetlands of the Northeast: Results of the National Wetlands Inventory. U.S. Fish and Wildlife Service, Northeast Region, Hadley, MA. 71 pp.

TABLE OF CONTENTS

List of Tables

(Note: See Appendix D for acreage summary tables for each state and the District of Columbia)

List of Figures

This page is intentionally blank

Executive Summary

The U.S. Fish and Wildlife Service established the National Wetlands Inventory (NWI) in the mid-1970s to map the nation's wetlands and deepwater habitats. Since then, the NWI has completed at least one phase of mapping for all northeastern states, except New York where roughly three-quarters of the state has been inventoried. For most areas, NWI maps have been converted to digital geospatial data which facilitates generation of acreage summaries of the NWI findings. State reports have been published for several states (Rhode Island, Connecticut, New Jersey, Delaware, and Maryland) and acreage summaries published for most other northeastern states. Since these reports were published, NWI data have been updated for many areas. This report summarizes current NWI data (as of September 2090) for each state from Maine through Virginia and the District of Columbia.

To date, nearly 9 million acres of wetlands have been inventoried by the NWI and are included in its national digital database. Three states had more than one million acres of wetlands: Maine (2.175M acres), New York (1.573M acres with only 74% of the state completed in digital format), and Virginia (1.471M acres). Wetland density (wetland acres/unit area) was highest in states dominated by the coastal plain - Delaware had the highest density of wetland with 21 percent of the state covered by wetland, followed closely by New Jersey with 20 percent. The presence of Chesapeake Bay and its tidal wetlands led to Virginia and Maryland being top-ranked in the acreage of tidal wetlands: Virginia with over 444,000 acres and Maryland with nearly 295,000 acres. New Jersey was the only other state with more than 250,000 acres of tidal wetlands. Estuarine emergent wetlands (salt and brackish marshes) were the predominant tidal wetland type in all coastal states except Maine where estuarine unconsolidated shores (tidal flats) were most common. Maine possessed the most palustrine wetland acreage with about 2 million acres mapped, whereas New York (based on digital wetland data for only 74% of the state) and Virginia both had over one million acres. Other states with more than 400,000 acres of these wetlands were New Jersey, Massachusetts, Maryland, and Pennsylvania. Forested wetlands were the dominant palustrine wetland type in all states, except in West Virginia where unconsolidated bottoms (ponds) were the most common type. Maine had the most acreage of forested and scrub-shrub wetlands mapped with over one million acres and nearly 550,000 acres, respectively.

In addition to creating NWI maps and geospatial data, the Region's NWI Program has produced a variety of other products including multi-state wetland trends reports, local inventory of wetland change reports, watershed-based wetland characterizations and preliminary functional assessments, and inventories of potential wetland restoration sites. These products plus the digital geospatial data and accompanying status reports have greatly increased our knowledge of the extent, distribution, and diversity of wetlands, their status and trends, wetland functions, and opportunities for their restoration. As such, the NWI has provided vital information to various Service programs, other federal agencies, state agencies, and others that has been used to help protect, conserve, and restore our nation's wetlands.

Acknowledgments

The National Wetlands Inventory (NWI) Program has been actively mapping the nation's wetlands since the mid-1970s and many people have contributed to the program's success. For the Northeast Region the actual mapping work was done mostly by a large cadre of photointerpreters and image analysts at the University of Massachusetts (Amherst, MA), the Conservation Management Institute of Virginia Tech University (Blacksburg, VA) and Regional NWI staff with hardcopy maps produced by the NWI Center at St. Petersburg, Florida. Key personnel that should be recognized for the interpretation work - the foundation for the NWI -include former Regional NWI staff - John Anderson, Herbert Bergquist, Anthony Davis, Gabriel DeAlessio, Kelly Drake, David Foulis, Joanne Gookin, Irene Huber, Todd Nuerminger, Sue Schaller, Matt Starr, and William Zinni, former UMass interpreters - chiefly Judy Harding, John LeBlanc, Meredith Borenstein, Kim Santos, Frank Shumway, Jennifer Silva, George Springston, and Janice Stone, and Virginia Tech staff - mainly Matt Fields, Nicole Furman, Kevin McGuckin, and Pamela Swint. Laura Roghair (Virginia Tech) provided analysis of the NWI database that was used to prepare the acreage summaries for this report. The NWI work over the past 35 years was done under the direction of Regional Wetland Coordinator Ralph Tiner with quality control support provided mainly by Assistant Coordinators John Organ, Glenn Smith, and John Swords. Peer review of this report was done by William Kirchner, Jo Ann Mills, John Swords, and Bill Wilen. Gina Jones prepared the report for final publication. Special thanks go to all these individuals plus the agencies and organizations that have contributed in various ways to the success of the NWI Program (Appendix A).

Introduction

The Northeast Region of the U.S. Fish and Wildlife Service has been actively mapping wetlands in thirteen states since the mid-1970s when the National Wetlands Inventory (NWI) Program was established. The NWI Program was created in 1974 to map the country's wetlands and provide the Service's biologists and others with information on the distribution and diversity of wetlands to aid in wetland conservation efforts. This was the first time that the federal government produced detailed maps showing the location of the diversity of wetlands that occur across the nation. The maps serve as invaluable aids for local planning and natural resource conservation.

The purpose of this report is three-fold to: (1) briefly describe the variety of activities performed by the Region's NWI Program, (2) increase awareness of the availability of regional NWI reports, and (3) present the findings of the NWI's 35 years worth of effort mapping wetlands in the Northeast.

Study Area

The Northeast Region encompasses thirteen states from Maine through Virginia including West Virginia. Major watersheds in the Region include the drainage basins of the Penobscot, Merrimack, Connecticut, Hudson, Delaware, Susquehanna, and Potomac Rivers. The Region also contains large coastal embayments including Chesapeake Bay (the largest estuary in the United States), Delaware Bay, and Long Island Sound plus the Gulf of Maine with its irregular rocky shoreline and marine-dominated ecosystems. From a physiographic perspective, the region ranges from the New England-Adirondack Highlands in the north to the Atlantic Coastal Plain, Piedmont, and Appalachian Highlands in the south, with the major ecosystems varying from boreal forests to broadleaf forests and pine or mixed pine/hardwood flatwoods (Figure 1). The Region contains a wealth of wetlands including boreal forested wetlands, bogs, fens, marshes, wet meadows, floodplain wetlands, coastal plain flatwoods, and tidal marshes (see Tiner 2005 for general descriptions of these types).

Figure 1. Ecoregions of the northeastern United States according to Bailey (1994).

212 – Laurentian Mixed Forest Province, M212 – Adirondack-New England Mixed Forest-Coniferous Forest-Alpine Meadow Province, 221 – Eastern Broadleaf Forest (Oceanic) Province, M221 – Central Appalachian Broadleaf Forest-Coniferous Forest-Meadow Province,

222 – Eastern Broadleaf Forest (Continental) Province, 231 – Southeastern Mixed Forest Province, and 232 – Outer Coastal Plain Mixed Forest Province.

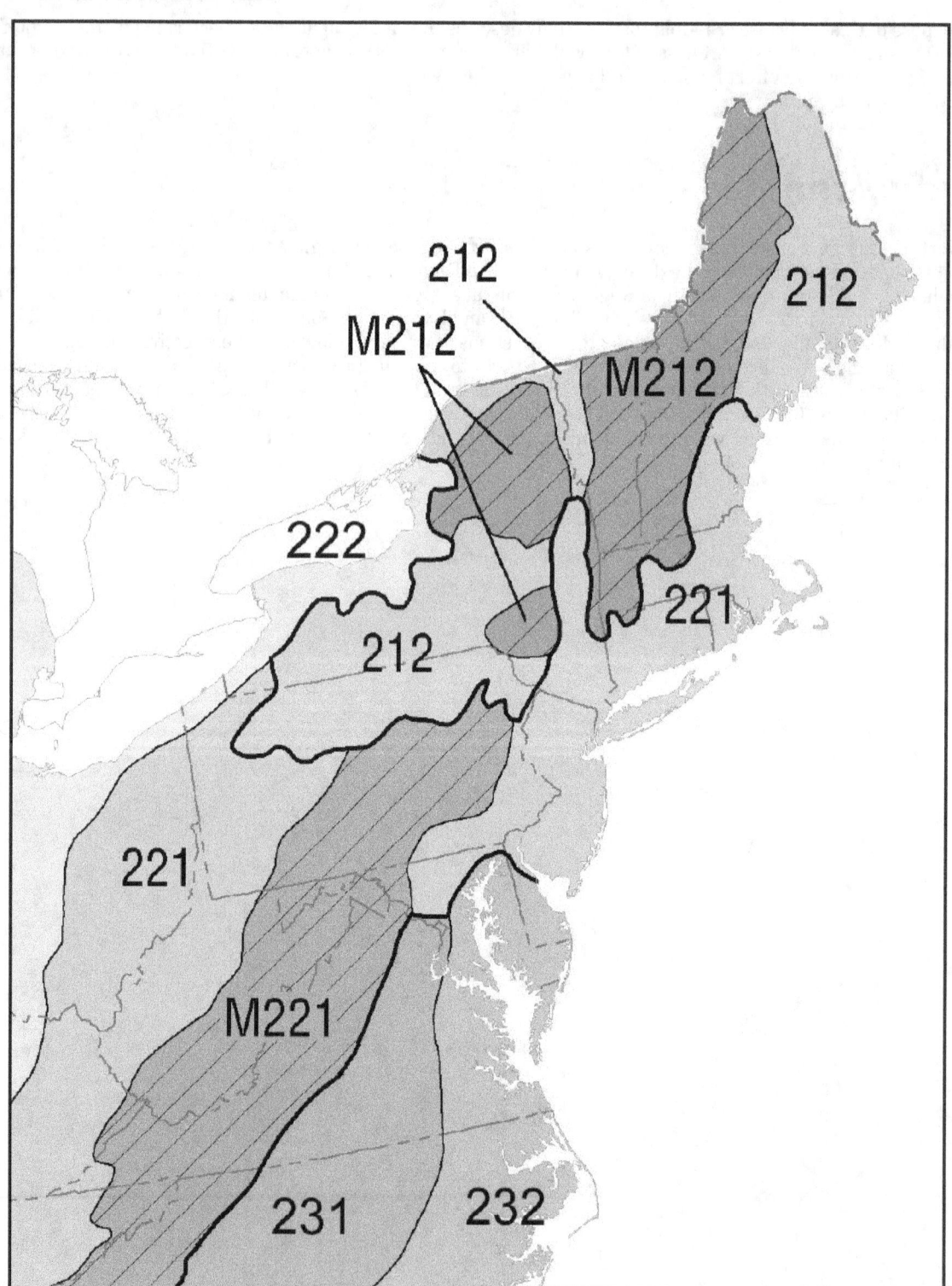

Overview of the Region's NWI Program

The Region's NWI Program is responsible for conducting the wetland inventory in thirteen northeastern states from Maine through Virginia. The main focus of this effort is to produce wetland maps (now geospatial data) following national standards established by the Program. Those standards have been recently adopted as the federal wetland mapping standard by the Federal Geographic Data Committee (FGDC 2009) for all federally-funded wetland mapping projects.[1] Besides the mapping, the Region's NWI Program performs studies to provide the Service and others with vital information to assist wetland conservation efforts. This work includes regional and local wetland change studies, watershed-based wetland characterizations, and landscape-level assessments of wetland functions.

Wetlands Inventory

The NWI employs conventional photointerpretation techniques upgraded to utilize modern-day computer technology to identify, classify, and delineate wetlands and deepwater habitats. This work is done by image analysts who interpret spectral signatures from aerial photographs or digital imagery, separate wetlands from deepwater habitats from uplands (dryland), delineate boundaries, and classify wetlands and deepwater habitats according to the federal government's official wetland classification system (Cowardin et al. 1979; an overview of this system is provided in Appendix B). Prior to the computer age and desktop mapping, the interpretations were recorded by pen and ink on an acetate overlay attached to an aerial photograph. The annotations were then compiled into map form by cartographers using zoom transfer scopes at the NWI Center in St. Petersburg, Florida. Maps were then digitized manually for computer applications. Today, the entire operation is done by image analysts on the computer using geographic information system (GIS) technology.

At the Program's inception, the NWI produced maps at a scale of 1:250,000 map (covering approximately 7,400 square miles). Service field personnel were not satisfied with this product so eventually large-scale (1:24,000) maps became the standard product (Figure 2). As computer mapping technology evolved, the NWI maps were digitized for GIS applications. In the mid-1990s, the NWI discontinued production of paper maps in favor of distributing NWI data via online "mapping tools" where people could make custom maps for their area of interest. Today, the NWI serves its data through a tool called the "Wetlands Mapper" which generates a planimeter map (Figure 3). NWI data can also be displayed on a topographic map via the U.S. Geological Survey's National Map (Figure 4) or on a current aerial image via a link to Google Earth. The general public can access and display NWI data using these tools. More sophisticated GIS users can connect their applications to real-time data directly through an online wetland mapping service or download NWI data for their own applications. Data can be downloaded by quad or by state. For an overview of the varied uses of NWI data, see "Status Report for the National Wetlands Inventory Program: 2009" (Tiner 2009: http://www.fws.gov/wetlands/_documents/gOther/StatusReportNWIProgram2009.pdf).

---

[1] This standard should be applied to all federal grants involving wetland mapping to insure that such mapping can be added to the NWI's wetlands master geospatial database.

Figure 2. Example of NWI map produced for Milton, Delaware.

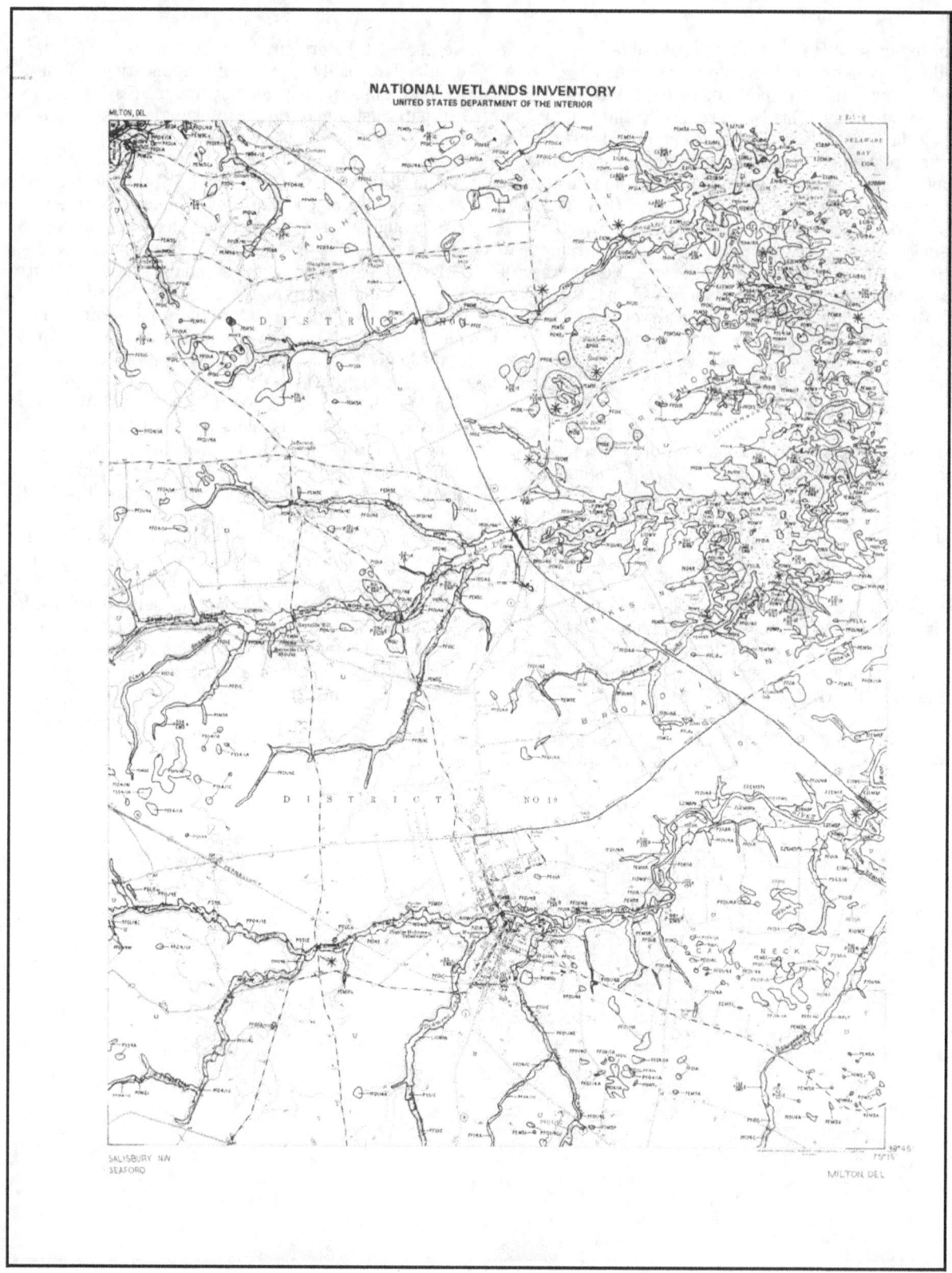

Figure 3. Custom NWI map for the Milton, Delaware area printed from the "Wetlands Mapper" showing a portion of the area covered in the previous figure.

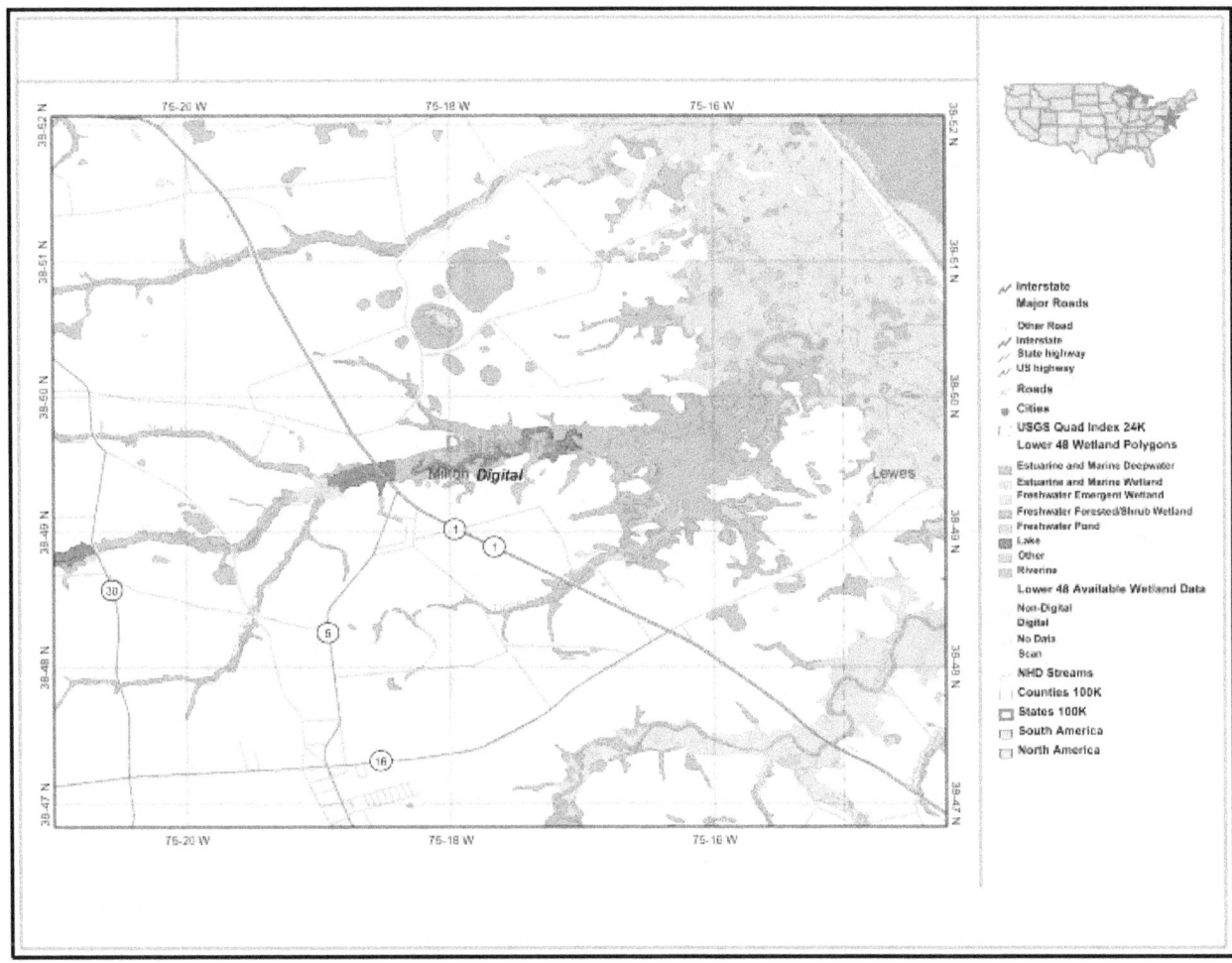

Figure 4. NWI data for the Milton, Delaware area printed on a topographic base from the U.S. Geological Survey's National Map.

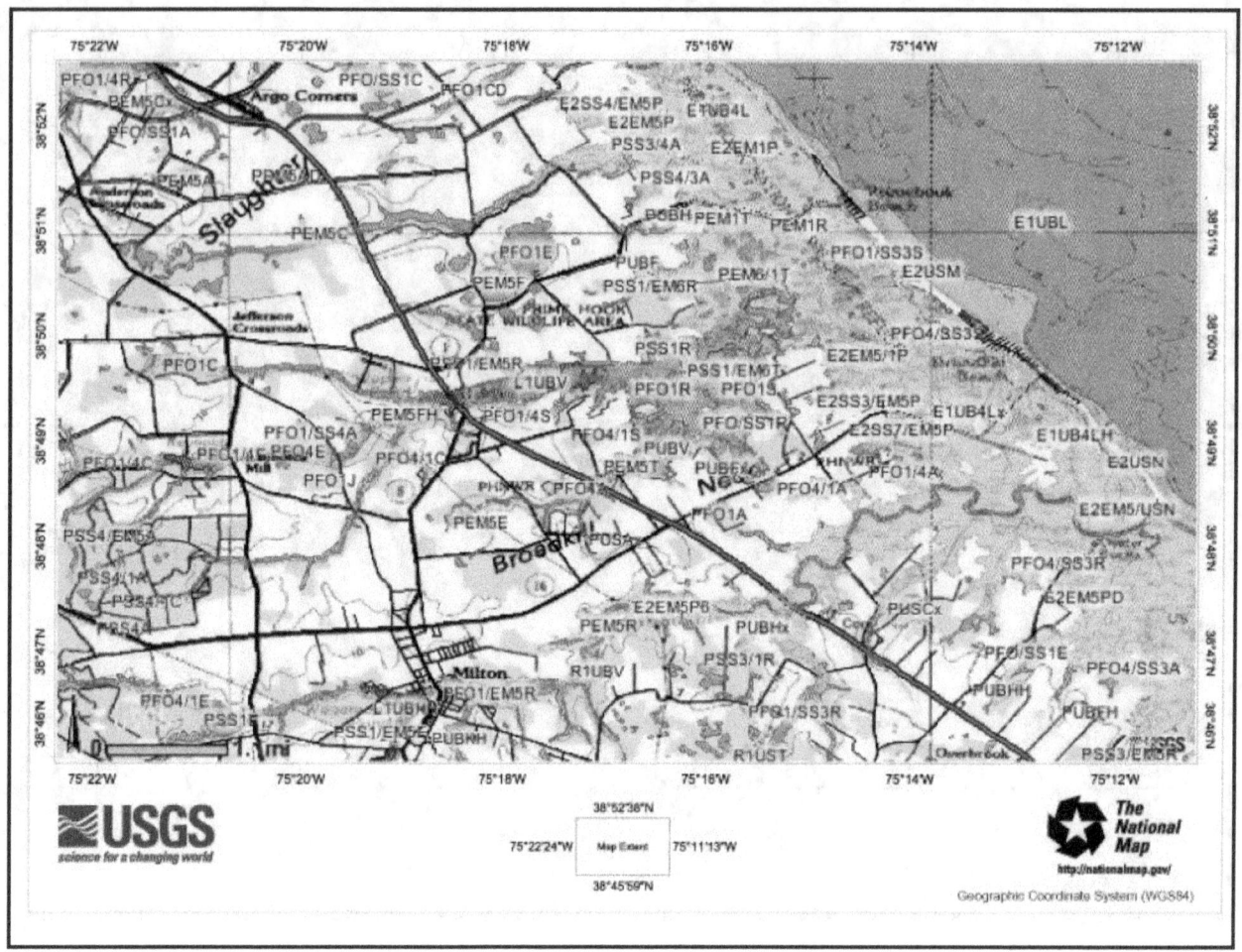

Special Projects

While wetland mapping remains the foundation of the NWI, the Region's NWI Program has produced a variety of ancillary products to expand the level of information provided by the program. These special projects have substantially added to our knowledge of Northeast wetlands.

Assessing Wetland Changes in the Region

Knowing how and why wetlands are changing is vital information for resource managers. The NWI employs two basic approaches for evaluating wetland changes: 1) statistically based probabilistic sampling and 2) inventory of change.[2] The former approach was developed for estimating status and trends of the nation's wetlands and involves analyzing changes in four-square mile plots (Frayer et al. 1983). The NWI has produced national reports on wetland status and trends using this approach since the 1980s (e.g., Tiner 1984 and Dahl 2006). This approach provides useful information for federal agency policy analysts but given its national focus is not as useful for guiding wetland conservation efforts at state and local levels. The Region used this approach for estimating trends in the five-state Mid-Atlantic region and the Chesapeake Bay watershed (e.g., Finn and Tiner 1986). The second approach – inventory of change – was developed by the Region's NWI Program for obtaining more detailed and area-specific information on the nature of local changes and the underlying causes than generated by the Service's national status and trends study. This approach does not produce estimates of changes, but instead is an inventory of wetland changes produced by comparing aerial imagery for the entire geographic area. Inventories of change have been performed for certain counties and smaller areas representing just a couple of 1:24K maps (see Appendix C for a list of these publications). This type of information is most useful for analyzing the effectiveness of government efforts to conserve and protect wetlands in specific geographic areas. As NWI data are updated in the Northeast, the Region's NWI Program plans to produce these inventories of change, as funding permits, to report on wetland changes for specific geographic areas as large as individual states.

Expanding NWI Data for Landscape-level Functional Assessment: NWIPlus

NWIPlus is an expanded database where other descriptors are added to the standard NWI database to improve its utility for preparing more detailed characterizations of wetland resources and for predicting wetland functions at the landscape level. In the 1970s and 1980s, the basic need for wetland data was inventory-based, that is, knowing where wetlands were on the landscape and how they differed in terms of vegetation type and hydrology. With strengthened wetland regulations since the late 1980s and early 1990s, another need surfaced - wetland functional assessment. As techniques were being developed for on-the-ground assessment of wetland functions, the Region's NWI Program sought ways to enhance its inventory so that landscape-level assessments of wetland functions could be derived from its database. To accomplish this, hydrogeomorphic-type descriptors were created to describe landscape position (i.e., the relationship between a wetland and a watercourse or waterbody if present), landform (the shape or physical form of a wetland), and water flow path (the directional flow of water). In addition, other descriptors were formulated to better address the diversity of waterbodies, especially for ponds, since every wetland trend study has shown an increase in pond acreage while vegetated wetlands declined. The type of pond and its landscape context provide important information for assessing pond functions. Collectively these descriptors are referred to as LLWW descriptors (landscape position, landform, water flow path, and waterbody type; Tiner 2003a). The NWI has worked with wetland specialists in the Northeast to develop correlations between wetland functions and the wetland characteristics recorded in the NWIPlus database (Tiner 2003b). These techniques have been used to produce watershed-based wetland characterizations and preliminary functional assessments for a number of watersheds in the Northeast (Table 1).[3] A list of available reports is given in Appendix C.

---

[2] Wetland change analysis is not done by comparing maps since maps produced during different stages of the inventory may not be comparable in quality. Image-to-image analysis produces a highly accurate and reliable assessment of wetland gains, losses, and changes in type for study areas. The NWI performs image-to-image analysis for identifying these changes.

[3] These techniques have been adopted by several states across the country for their wetland inventories and for utilizing existing wetland data to predict wetland functions (see article in forthcoming May-June 2010 issue of the National Wetlands Newsletter).

Table 1. Geographic areas where NWIPlus data have been created or are planned for 2010-11. A report characterizing wetlands and their functions was produced or is planned for most areas.

State	Geographic Area
Maine	Casco Bay watershed
Massachusetts	Boston Harbor area, Cape Cod, Nantucket, and Martha's Vineyard
Rhode Island	Entire state
Connecticut	Entire state (in progress)
New York	Long Island (in progress); New York City water supply watersheds; eleven small watersheds across the state: Catherine Creek, Cumberland Bay, Hudson River-Snook Kill, Peconic River, Post Creek to Sing Sing Creek, Salmon River to South Sandy Creek, Sodus Bay to Wolcott Creek, Sodus Creek, Sucker Brook to Grass River, Upper Tioughnioga River, and Upper Wappinger Creek
New Jersey	Entire state (in progress)
Delaware	Nanticoke watershed, entire state (in progress)
Maryland	Nanticoke watershed, Coastal Bays watershed

Potential Wetland Restoration Site Mapping

Another area of growing interest in wetland conservation is wetland restoration. In the early 1990s, the Region's NWI Program worked with the Massachusetts Executive Office of Environmental Affair's Wetlands Restoration and Banking Program and the University of Massachusetts on special projects designed to identify potential wetland restoration sites for some of the state's watersheds. At that time, the Massachusetts Wetlands Restoration and Banking Program applied a watershed-based wetland restoration approach aimed at targeting wetland restoration in strategic locations that could help alleviate watershed problems (e.g., flood damages, degraded water quality, and fragmented wildlife habitat). The NWI assisted in developing this approach which ultimately gave the NWI Program the vision and capability for producing potential wetland restoration site inventories. Potential wetland restoration sites include former wetlands that have been drained or filled but are still in a condition where restoration is possible (Type 1 restoration sites) and existing wetlands that have functions impaired by ditching, excavation, impoundment, or cultivation (Type 2 restoration sites). The former sites are identified using soil maps and locating hydric soil areas that are not mapped as NWI wetlands and do not have any buildings or other structures built upon them. These restoration site inventories are now often part of watershed-based wetland inventories and functional assessments as the data used in these investigations make it easy to document potential restoration sites. Through the watershed assessments, it is also possible to identify sites for possible restoration of streamside (riparian) vegetation. Depending on project funding and objectives, the Region's NWI Program is attempting to include wetland restoration site inventories as part of its standard NWI updating procedures.

Assessing Natural Habitat Integrity for Watersheds

Looking beyond wetlands to the entire watershed is important to assess the "health" of wetlands and waters since activities in the surrounding landscape significantly affect water quality and habitat quality of wetlands. The condition of wetland and stream buffers is particularly important for wetland and aquatic wildlife. The widespread availability of land use/cover geospatial data made it possible to integrate NWI data with these data to evaluate and report on the condition of natural habitat surrounding wetlands and waterbodies and for watersheds as a whole. To accomplish this, the Region's NWI Program developed a set of "natural habitat integrity indices" that can be used for reporting on the condition of natural habitats for large geographic areas – a suite of useful metrics for an environmental report card (Tiner 2004). Thirteen indices were created: seven addressing habitat extent (i.e., the amount of natural habitat occurring in the watershed and along wetlands and waterbodies), four dealing with habitat disturbances (emphasizing human-induced alterations to streams, wetlands, and terrestrial habitats), and one composite index. The eight "natural habitat extent indices" are natural cover, river corridor integrity, stream corridor integrity, vegetated wetland buffer integrity, pond buffer integrity, lake buffer integrity, wetland extent, and standing waterbody extent. The four "habitat disturbance indices@ involve dammed stream flowage, channelized stream flowage, wetland disturbance, and habitat fragmentation by roads. The last index - "composite natural habitat integrity index" – may be calculated in two ways: one is comprised of the weighted sum of the habitat extent indices minus the sum of the disturbance indices (weighted composite natural habitat integrity index), while the alternative is a simple sum of the extent indices minus the sum of the disturbance indices (simple summed composite natural habitat integrity index). These indices were intended to augment, not supplant, other more rigorous, fine-filter approaches for describing the ecological condition of watersheds and for examining relationships between human impacts and natural resources. The indices can be used as one metric for an environmental report card that addresses the changing quality of lands and waters in specific geographic regions. NWI has applied the indices to special projects funded by the Service or state agencies interested in assessing the overall condition of natural habitat for individual watersheds (e.g., Tiner and Bergquist 2007). An adjacent Service region (Great Lakes Region, Region 3) has also applied these indices to their entire region to produce a map of watershed health (Figure 5), while the states of Montana and Virginia have adapted these indices for assessing their watersheds (e.g., Vance et al. 2009, Ciminelli and Scrivani 2007).

Figure 5. Application of natural habitat integrity indices to Midwest states by U.S. Fish and Wildlife Service, Region 3, Division of Conservation Planning. (<u>Note</u>: This is an early version of the application, contact the Region for the latest edition.)

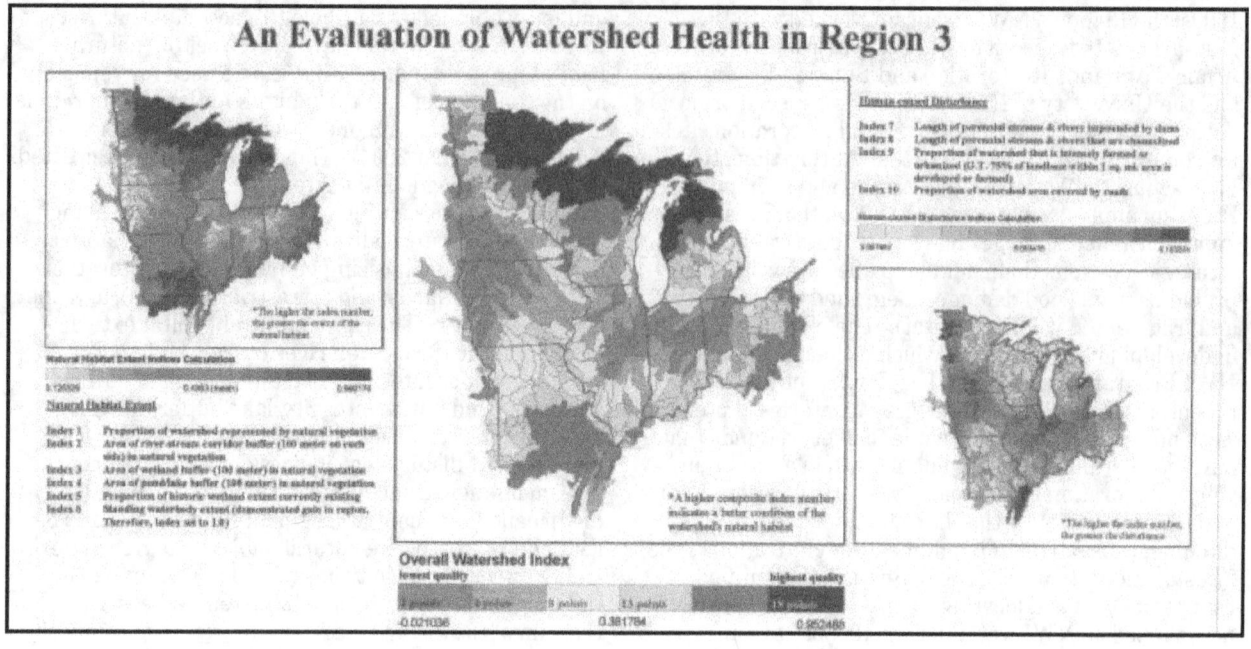

NWI Mapping for the Northeast

The NWI has complete coverage of wetland data for all Northeast states except New York. Some areas have been updated once or twice since the NWI was initiated in the mid-1970s and state reports have been published in one form or another for all states except Massachusetts, Vermont, New York, and Virginia, although preliminary statistics based on the original mapping were published for the former two states (see publications list, Appendix C). Readers should recognize that an inventory is not a one-time mapping effort, but instead it is an ongoing process because wetlands are changing due to both natural forces and human activities. Also advances in mapping technology make it possible to improve the accuracy and completeness of the inventory. New data have been added to the database for many states, making the previous acreage summaries reported by NWI obsolete. The most recent findings are reported in the last major section of this report "Extent of Wetlands and Deepwater Habitats in the Northeast."

Current Status of Mapping

The status of NWI mapping for the Region as of September 2009 is shown in Figure 6. This report summarizes NWI acreage data where digital data are available (green areas) as data for other areas are either not available (pink) or only available in hardcopy maps (tan areas).

The effective date of the NWI across the Region is shown in Figure 7. NWI data are derived not from a single time period as funding and imagery constraints make this impossible. While most of the data are from the mid-1980s (green areas), some of the data are from the 1970s (purple areas) and many areas have been recently updated (blue and red areas). In some areas of the region, development is not occurring at a rapid pace and therefore the mid-1980s data may still reflect current conditions. The program continues to work in priority areas.

Figure 6. Status of the NWI in the Northeast Region as of September 2009. Non-digital means only hardcopy maps are available. The data summaries presented in this report were derived from the areas shown in green on this map.

Figure 7. Era of imagery for NWI mapping for the Northeast Region as of September 2009.

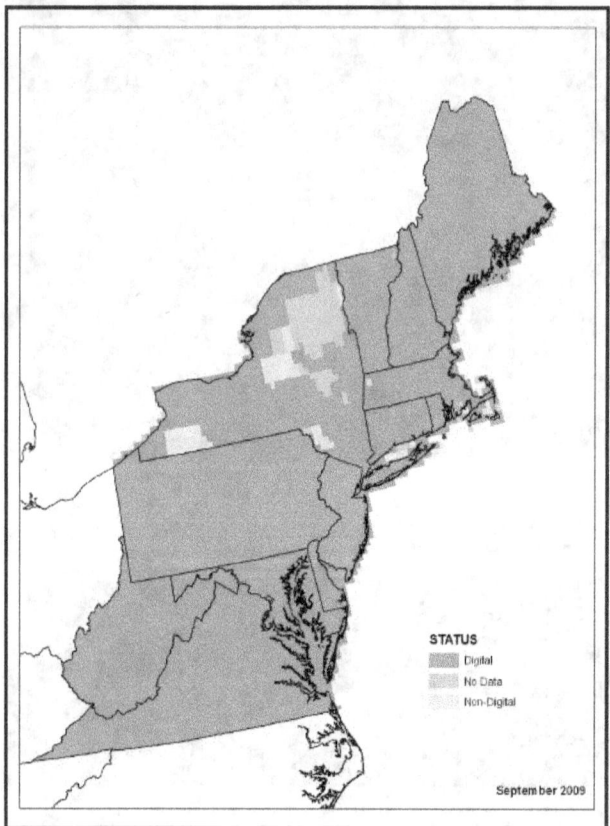

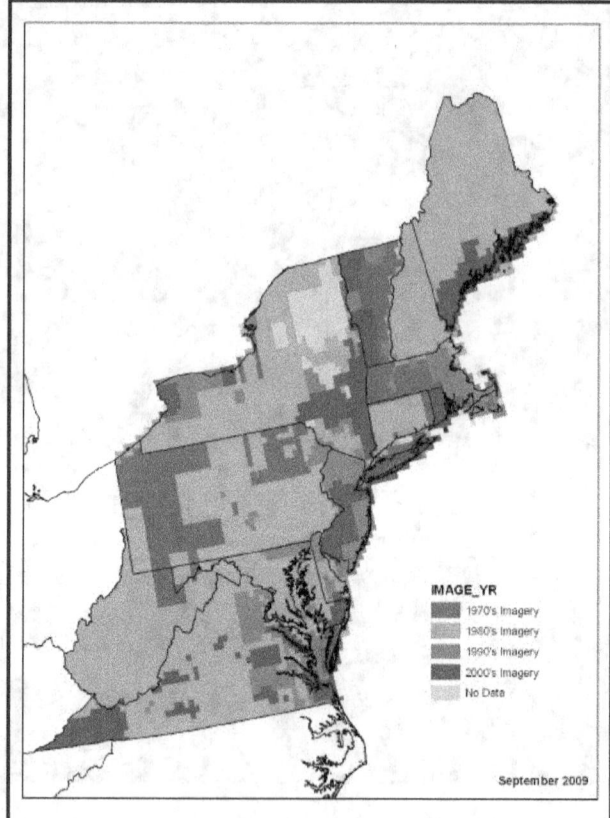

Mapping Limitations

The mapping techniques of the NWI have evolved over time. NWI mapping has improved for a number of reasons including the availability of higher resolution imagery, advances in GIS technology, the ability to integrate NWI data with other geospatial data sources, and standardized techniques for wetland identification and delineation. With any mapping effort, there are limitations due to scale, image quality, and other factors. Given these considerations, it is impossible to map every wetland and NWI data are no exception. Some limitations of NWI mapping are identified in Table 2. The data presented in this report were derived from mapping performed using a variety of imagery sources and during times where our knowledge of wetlands grew exponentially.

The source imagery affects a number of factors in wetland mapping: scale (related to smallest wetland that can be mapped), the emulsion (ability to detect wetlands), the timing (seasonality affects ability to detect and classify wetlands), and the date (relates to the currentness of the inventory, especially in rapidly developing areas). Since the NWI utilized different imagery during the course of the inventory, the date of the imagery used in preparing the NWI can be used to interpret the mapping detail as follows (Figure 7). The 1970s imagery (1:80,000 black and white aerial photography) generally yields a target mapping unit (tmu) of 3-5 acres. This means that most wetlands larger than this size range should be mapped, while smaller wetlands are not consistently shown due to scale issues. The black and white film also is not as useful for detecting wetlands as color infrared film, so wetland mapping is more conservative. The 1980s imagery (typically 1:58,000 color infrared photography) allows for a tmu of 1-3 acres in size, whereas the tmu for the 1990s imagery (1:40,000 color infrared photography) is about 1 acre. The 2000-era imagery is digital imagery of varying levels of resolution, but is equivalent or better than the 1:40K photography. The tmu for this imagery is ½ acre. A drawback for some of the 2000-era imagery is that it is sometimes true color rather than color infrared. True color imagery is not as reliable for detecting wetlands as color infrared. However, when interpreting the 2000-era imagery, existing NWI data are usually being updated, so the original data derived from color infrared aerial photography plus the on-screen mapping process allow the analyst to simultaneously view USDA soil mapping with the net outcome being an improved wetland map.

While Figure 7 shows the general timeframe of the imagery, it does not indicate the season in which the imagery was acquired. Leaf-off imagery is best for wetland detection. In some areas, such imagery was not available for the NWI, so leaf-on imagery was used (e.g., central and western Pennsylvania). For these areas, NWI produced a rather conservative inventory as many forested wetlands were not detectable. When using NWI data posted online on the Wetlands Mapper (http://www.fws.gov/wetlands/Data/Mapper.html), readers should read the accompanying metadata (click on "Wetland Project Area Metadata") to learn the specific date of the imagery used. If summer imagery was the primary source, the NWI data will be quite conservative. In any event, when using NWI to determine whether or not wetland is present on a given parcel of land, individuals are encouraged to also consult the U.S. Department of Agriculture's web soil survey for the presence of "hydric soils" (http://websoilsurvey.nrcs.usda.gov/app/HomePage.htm).

Table 2. Some limitations of NWI data. (Adapted from Tiner 1999)

1. Target mapping unit (tmu). A tmu is an estimate of the minimum-sized wetland that the NWI is attempting to map and is largely dependent on photo/image scale. Conspicuous wetlands smaller than the tmu (especially ponds) are often included in the inventory.

2. Aquatic bed mapping. Since spring (leaf-off) imagery was typically used by the NWI, aquatic beds were not visible since plants are just beginning to grow at this time and plant parts are well beneath the water's surface. When observed in the field, boundaries of these beds were approximated, but typically aquatic beds were included within the waterbody classification – usually the unconsolidated bottom class.

3. Excessive flooding on imagery. In some cases, extreme high water conditions obscured the life form of the vegetation. While in many cases, vegetation could be observed underwater, determining whether it was herbaceous or low-growing shrubs was difficult. Consequently, some shrub wetlands may have been classified as emergent wetlands and vice versa.

4. Use of leaf-on imagery. In central and western Pennsylvania, leaf-on imagery was the only imagery available for the NWI and resulted in a conservative wetlands inventory as many forested wetlands could not be detected on this imagery. For the rest of the region, leaf-off imagery was typically available.

5. Temporarily flooded and seasonally saturated forested wetlands. These wetlands occur on higher portions of floodplains or on nearly level broad plains such as the coastal plain (New Jersey south) or glaciolactustrine plain (e.g., western New York – former shoreline of Great Lakes). They are among the more difficult wetlands to interpret especially when dominated by evergreen species. USDA soil survey data have been used to help interpret these areas. NWI data collected prior to 1989 may not show many of these areas. Availability of digital soils data since then has facilitated identification of these areas based on the presence of hydric soils.

6. Estuarine wetlands, freshwater tidal wetlands, and tidal waters. Delineation of the break between estuarine and riverine tidal systems and the oligohaline (slightly brackish) segment of estuaries were based on a combination of limited field observations, image interpretation, and published reports. The boundaries should be considered approximate. Some tidal swamps may be classified as nontidal forested wetlands where the upper limit of tidal influence was not mapped to its maximum upstream penetration.

7. Tidal flats. Since the photos were not synchronized to capture low tide conditions, all tidal flats were not visible on the imagery used. The boundaries of tidal flats were approximated from coastal and geodetic survey maps and topopgraphic maps when necessary. Recognize that some of these features, especially sand flats, are dynamic and current locations and boundaries may be different than those depicted on the maps or in the digital database, especially after major storm events (e.g., hurricanes).

8. Tidal marshes. Identification of high marsh (irregularly flooded) versus low marsh (regularly flooded) is conservative. Most marshes were identified as high marsh and some low marsh may be included in this type.

9. Water regimes. These hydrologic characteristics were determined based on spectral signatures on the imagery coupled with findings from limited field investigations. Long-term hydrologic studies would improve the results but were beyond the scope of the NWI. On the coastal plain and glaciolacustrine plains, the "B" water regime (saturated) was applied to areas that are seasonally saturated. Note: The earliest NWI mapping applied the temporarily flooded water regime to these wetlands, but it was later felt that the saturated water regime would better reflect site wetness brought about by seasonal high water tables from winter to early spring and not by inundation (i.e., ponding in micro-depressions).

10. Farmed wetlands. In the Northeast, the early NWI mapping tended to limit farmed wetlands to cultivated cranberry bogs due to the ease of their identification. Later, the NWI also mapped depressional wetlands in cultivated fields as farmed wetlands based on their appearance on aerial imagery. Overall, farmed wetlands are conservatively mapped by the NWI and the actual acreage of such areas is greater than cited in this report. Determination of farmed wetlands in areas subject to drainage typically would require a more detailed assessment of their hydrology for accurate identification.

11. Linear wetlands. Long, narrow wetlands that follow drainageways and stream corridors may or may not be mapped depending on project objectives. Although the hardcopy NWI maps showed these areas, NWI's online mapping tool - Wetlands Mapper - does not display such features at this time.

12. Inclusion of uplands. Small upland features may be included within mapped wetland boundaries due to image scale. Field inspections and analysis of more detailed imagery may be used to identify such features.

The National Wetlands Database

The database used to generate the acreage summaries for this report is maintained by the National Wetlands Inventory's National Support and Standards Team (Madison, WI). Wetland geospatial data for this report were entered into the national database prior to September 2009. The data for Northeast wetlands were produced exclusively by the Region's NWI Program.[4] Data summaries were generated from the polygonal data in the database (no linear data were analyzed) by GIS specialists at Virginia Tech's Conservation Management Institute (Blacksburg, VA). Data were summarized for states, counties, and hydrologic units (HUC-4 and HUC-8 units). Data presented in this report refer only to the state totals (acreages of wetlands and deepwater habitats by major type). Data for the other groupings are available on a limited basis upon request: contact Ralph Tiner at ralph_tiner@fws.gov. In the future, these data may be posted online.

Aggregating Wetland Types for This Report

Due to the classification hierarchy that includes system, subsystem, class, subclass, water regime, and other modifiers, there are thousands of combinations possible. To simplify the data for this report, data were aggregated at the class level. In compiling this regional summary, mixed classes were assigned to the dominant class (e.g., PFO1/SS1C was included in the forested wetland category - PFO, while PSS1/FO1C was placed in scrub-shrub type - PSS). Marine, Estuarine, Lacustrine and Palustrine wetlands can be readily identified by the NWI code (i.e., M2___, E2___, L2___ and P____, respectively). While some Riverine wetland types can be clearly identified as wetland by consulting the class level – unconsolidated shore, rocky shore, or streambed (intermittent) – or by water regime (not permanently flooded), open water Riverine wetlands are not easily recognized since shallow water habitats are not separated from deep water ones – all are classified either rock bottom or unconsolidated bottom. Consequently, all permanently flooded rivers and streams (rock bottom and unconsolidated bottom) were placed in the deepwater habitat category for these summaries. The only exception to this was where the bottom type was mixed with emergent wetland. The presence of this vegetation suggests that the area is a shallow water wetland. This was a rare occurrence. If the open water area was mixed with aquatic bed vegetation, its acreage was included in the deepwater habitat summaries since such vegetation can grow in deep water or as a floating mat in slow-flowing rivers and streams.

Interpretation of Results

The numbers presented in this report represent the best available wetland acreage estimates for the areas completed by the NWI as of September 2009. They reflect the tabular results of 35-years of mapping by the program (see Figure 7 for effective inventory date based on imagery used). For coastal states, the marine acreage does not reflect the full extent of state waters as NWI data only go to the limits of the most seaward U.S. Geological Survey topographic map. Statewide NWI data are not complete for three states in the region (Table 3). The numbers presented for New York represent the findings for about three-quarters of the state (i.e., digital wetland data). Although NWI completed wetland mapping for Massachusetts and Vermont, digital data for a few quads have not been produced. The findings for these states, however, represent more than 98 percent of the states. Readers should refer to Figure 6 to see what parts of these three states the summary data reflect. Farmed wetlands are not consistently mapped and in all states, the extent of farmed wetlands is probably larger than given in this report. Another important point is that since data are added to the database periodically, the acreage of wetlands mapped will change overtime. For the latest acreage, individuals may want to download NWI data for a state and generate acreage summaries. For information on updates since September 2009, contact contact Ralph Tiner, Regional Wetland Coordinator at ralph_tiner@fws.gov

---

[4] The national database also includes FGDC-compliant wetland data produced by other organizations, but to date, there are no such data from northeastern states. In the near future, however, the state of Delaware will be submitting such data for Kent and New Castle Counties.

Table 3. Type and coverage of NWI data for each Northeast state and the District of Columbia as of September 2009. The number represents the % of area covered by the data type.

NWI Data Type

State	Digital Data	Hardcopy Maps Only	No Data
Connecticut	100.0	--	--
Delaware	100.0	--	--
District of Columbia	100.0	--	--
Maine	100.0	--	--
Maryland	100.0	--	--
Massachusetts	98.0	2.0	--
New Hampshire	100.0	--	--
New Jersey	100.0	--	--
New York	73.9	9.7	16.4
Pennsylvania	100.0	--	--
Rhode Island	100.0	--	--
Vermont	99.2	0.8	--
Virginia	100.0	--	--
West Virginia	100.0	--	--

Extent of Wetlands and Deepwater Habitats in the Northeast

The results of the 35-year effort by the NWI are summarized for the region in a series of tables and Appendix D. The first two tables (Tables 4 and 5) give wetland and deepwater totals according to ecological system for each state and the District of Columbia. Table 6 shows the percent of the state's land area that was occupied by wetland. Tables 7 and 8 address the dominant types of tidal and palustrine wetlands across the region. More detailed tabular summaries for each state and the District of Columbia are given in Appendix D. These tables include the acreage of specific types of wetland and deepwater habitat mapped (to the class level).

Note: Remember that NWI data were not complete for three states: New York, Massachusetts, and Vermont, so the results do not represent statewide totals (Table 3; Figure 6). For New York, digital NWI data were available for 74 percent of the state. For Massachusetts and Vermont, a few NWI maps were not digitized, so the results for these states are based on 98 percent and 99 percent coverage, respectively.

Northeastern states with more than one-half million acres of wetland were Maine (2.175M acres), New York (1.573M acres for 73.9% of the state mapped by NWI), Virginia (1.471M acres), New Jersey 0.937M acres), Maryland (0.701M acres), and Massachusetts (0.536M acres) (Table 4). Mountainous West Virginia and Rhode Island, the smallest state in the nation, had the least wetland acreage.

Five states had more than one million acres of deepwater habitat mapped (Table 5). New York had the most acreage due to the presence of Lake Ontario, Long Island Sound, Peconic Bay, other coastal waters behind its barrier islands (e.g., Jones Beach Island and Fire Island), and marine waters offshore. Maine was second-ranked and had the most marine acreage due to the Gulf of Maine (e.g., Penobscot and Casco Bays), while Virginia with the bulk of Chesapeake Bay was third-ranked.

Delaware had the highest density of wetland per land area with 21 percent of the state represented by wetland (Table 6). New Jersey was a close second with about 20 percent coverage by wetland. Other states with more than 10 percent of their land area occupied by wetland were Maryland, Maine, Massachusetts, and Rhode Island.

The presence of Chesapeake Bay and its tidal wetlands led to Virginia and Maryland being top-ranked in the acreage of tidal wetlands (Table 7). Virginia was first-ranked with over 444,000 acres mapped, while Maryland possessed nearly 295,000 acres. New Jersey was third-ranked with more than 250,000 acres of tidal wetlands, followed by Maine with almost 168,000 acres. Estuarine emergent wetlands (salt and brackish marshes) were the predominant tidal wetland type in all coastal states except Maine where estuarine unconsolidated shores (tidal flats) were most common. Maine with its irregular rocky shoreline had the most acreage of marine wetlands, comprising about 65 percent of the entire region's marine wetlands (Table 4). Rocky shore and unconsolidated wetlands were the predominant marine wetland type in Maine, whereas unconsolidated shore (intertidal beaches and tidal flats) was the most common type in other states (Table 7).

Palustrine wetlands (freshwater marshes, swamps, bogs, and ponds) were the most abundant general wetland type in all states (Table 4). Maine had the most palustrine wetland acreage with about 2 million acres mapped, while New York and Virginia both had over one million acres. When the NWI is completed for New York that state might end up with the greatest palustrine wetland acreage. Currently with 74 percent of the state mapped, 1.5 million acres were reported and if the acreage in the unmapped portion of the state has at least the same wetland density as the rest of the state, New York will have over 2 million acres and slightly more than was mapped in Maine. Other states with more than 400,000 acres of these wetlands were, in order of abundance: New Jersey, Massachusetts, Maryland, and Pennsylvania. Forested wetlands were the dominant palustrine wetland type in all states, except in West Virginia where unconsolidated bottoms (ponds) were the most common type (Table 8). Maine had the most acreage of forested and scrub-shrub wetlands mapped with over one million acres and nearly 550,000 acres, respectively. New York was second-ranked in both forested and scrub-shrub wetland acreage, in spite of the fact that the data represent only 74 percent of the state. Virginia was third-ranked in all categories of palustrine vegetated wetlands and second-ranked in pond acreage (unconsolidated bottom). New York had the most acreage of both palustrine emergent wetlands, unconsolidated bottom wetlands (ponds), and farmed wetlands. New Jersey was second-ranked in farmed wetlands due to the extent of cranberry cultivation, followed by Massachusetts (another cranberry-producing state) and Delaware.

Table 4. Wetland acreage for northeastern states and the District of Columbia based on NWI data as of September 2009. *Note that NWI digital data for New York covers 74% of the state; see Figure 6 for location of mapped area where digital data are available.

Acreage Summaries

	Marine	Estuarine	Palustrine	Lacustrine	Riverine	Total Wetlands	Rank
Connecticut	--	18,788	181,286	1,513	292	201,879	11
Delaware	622	83,082	178,885	54	434	263,077	10
District of Columbia	--	--	237	27	149	413	14
Maine	69,816	83,175	2,000,893	16,495	4,753	2,175,132	1
Maryland	722	248,214	448,214	1,415	1,951	700,516	5
Massachusetts	21,269	61,854	450,114	2,974	168	536,379	6
New Hampshire	886	9,297	280,234	698	1,455	292,570	8
New Jersey	4,224	208,713	719,991	784	3,274	936,986	4
New York	4,983	36,161	1,485,846	39,637	6,126	1,572,753	2
Pennsylvania	--	55	420,118	8,809	3,665	432,647	7
Rhode Island	930	7,288	62,454	6	--	70,678	12
Vermont	--	--	240,464	22,437	482	263,383	9
Virginia	4,377	350,189	1,108,015	4,393	3,738	1,470,712	3
West Virginia	--	--	54,406	2,550	1,442	58,398	13
Totsl	107,829	1,106,816	7,631,157	101,792	27,929	8,975,523	

Table 5. Deepwater habitat acreage for northeastern states and the District of Columbia based on NWI data as of September 2009. *Note that NWI digital data for New York covers 74% of the state; see Figure 6 for mapped area where digital data are available.

Acreage Summaries

	Marine	Estuarine	Lacustrine	Riverine	Total	Rank
Connecticut	--	349,005	36,341	14,683	400,029	8
Delaware	54,873	271,779	4,176	4,249	335,077	9
District of Columbia	--	--	319	3,944	4,263	14
Maine	1,345,872	78,937	922,796	92,294	2,439,899	2
Maryland	57,415	1,541,510	20,956	38,633	1,658,514	4
Massachusetts	1,048,892	97,459	124,478	21,564	1,292,393	5
New Hampshire	42,842	7,711	166,859	19,677	237,089	12
New Jersey	308,601	508,179	50,594	26,670	894,044	6
New York	785,899	847,238	1,174,581	145,227	2,952,945	1
Pennsylvania	--	647	312,209	170,731	483,587	7
Rhode Island	172,630	88,390	19,484	1,079	281,583	10
Vermont	--	--	199,426	13,341	212,767	11
Virginia	258,673	1,362,007	139,669	146,736	1,907,085	3
West Virginia	--	--	17,089	91,012	108,101	13
Totsl	4,075,697	5,152,862	3,188,977	789,840	13,207,376	

Table 6. Percent of land area mapped as wetland by the NWI. Land area comes from U.S. Census 2000 data as reported by Wikipedia.org. http://simple.wikipedia.org/wiki/List_of_U.S._states_by_area

	Land Area (sq. mi.)	% Wetland	Rank
Connecticut	4,845	6.5	8
Delaware	1,954	21.0	1
District of Columbia	61	1.1	13
Maine	30,862	11.0	4
Maryland	9,774	11.2	3
Massachusetts	7,840	10.9*	5
New Hampshire	8,968	5.1	10
New Jersey	7,417	19.7	2
New York	47,214	7.0*	7
Pennsylvania	44,817	1.5	12
Rhode Island	1,045	10.6	6
Vermont	9,250	4.5*	11
Virginia	39,594	5.8	9
West Virginia	24,078	0.4	14

NWI digital data does not cover entire state; percent based on NWI acreage versus proportion of state mapped (MA – 98.0%, NY – 73.9%, and VT – 99.2%).

Table 7. Acreage of major tidal wetland types across the region. Note: Freshwater tidal wetlands are represented by Palustrine and Riverine types. Coding: US – Unconsolidated Shore, RS – Rocky Shore, EM – Emergent, FO – Forested, SS – Scrub-Shrub.

	Marine			Estuarine			Palustrine (tidal)				Riverine		
	US	RS	Other	EM	US	Other	EM	FO	SS	Other	EM/US*	Total Area	Rank
Connecticut	–	–	–	12,128	6,393	267	1,225	50	349	45	251	20,708	8
Delaware	622	–	–	77,256	4,880	946	3,229	5,520	1,550	715	434	95,152	5
District of Columbia	–	–	–	–	–	–	7	79	1	2	141	230	12
Maine	26,407	30,141	13,268	22,539	51,620	9,016	2,203	6,144	3,508	405	2,420	167,671	4
Maryland	722	–	–	205,184	23,670	19,360	3,955	39,960	2,926	250	1,750	294,777	2
Massachusetts	19,488	825	956	44,894	15,501	1,459	1,182	1,808	1,483	352	6	87,954	6
New Hampshire	500	161	225	5,904	3,273	120	110	520	164	60	–	11,037	9
New Jersey	4,224	12	–	201,837	5,154	1,722	10,557	18,870	10,584	890	2,731	256,569	3
New York	4,957	18	8	27,684	7,074	1,403	1,558	2,570	499	230	440	46,441	7
Pennsylvania	–	–	–	–	55	–	200	220	13	46	917	1,451	11
Rhode Island	714	215	1	3,678	3,419	191	34	94	16	33	–	8,395	10
Virginia	4,285	–	92	197,335	143,789	9,065	21,839	56,238	8,123	771	2,547	444,084	1

*Acreage is mostly emergent and unconsolidated shore wetland but may include a few acres of minor types (see state tables in Appendix D for details).

Table 8. Acreage of major palustrine wetland types across the region. Note: Includes freshwater tidal palustrine wetlands.

	Emergent	Forested	Scrub-Shrub	Unconsolidated Bottom	Other	Total	Rank
Connecticut	12,613	106,463	27,818	34,135	257	181,286	10
Delaware	11,805	146,412	13,163	3,780	3,725*	178,885	11
District of Columbia	12	183	9	23	10	237	14
Maine	200,952	1,194,848	547,999	55,658	1,436*	2,000,893	1
Maryland	33,958	359,897	35,932	16,649	1,778*	448,214	6
Massachusetts	39,682	293,268	84,562	26,983	5,619*	450,114	5
New Hampshire	39,452	140,451	73,984	26,101	246	280,234	8
New Jersey	67,314	515,951	102,610	27,782	6,334*	719,991	4
New York	219,944	892,019	257,411	92,773	23,699*	1,485,846	2
Pennsylvania	59,023	219,101	79,589	60,452	1,953	420,118	7
Rhode Island	3,051	48,665	5,887	4,680	171*	62,454	12
Vermont	47,222	117,801	59,947	13,717	1,777*	240,464	9
Virginia	107,743	811,100	103,902	82,291	2,979*	1,108,015	3
West Virginia	13,623	12,762	11,198	16,486	337	54,406	13

*Includes farmed wetlands: 3,370 acres in DE, 491 acres in ME (including 307 acres of cultivated cranberry bogs), 662 acres in MD, 4,528 acres in MA (including 4,473 acres of cranberry bogs), 7,401 acres in NJ (including 4,590 acres of cranberry bogs), 21,731 acres in NY, 107 acres in RI (cranberry bogs), 1,114 acres in VT, and 1,171 acres in VA.

Summary

Since the mid-1970s, the U.S. Fish and Wildlife Service's NWI Program has completed at least one phase of mapping for all northeastern states, except New York. Most of the region has NWI data in digital form that allowed generation of acreage summaries of the NWI findings for each state and the District of Columbia. To date, nearly 9 million acres of wetlands have been mapped and included in the NWI digital database. Three states had more than one million acres of wetlands recorded: Maine (2.175M acres), New York (1.573M acres with only 74% of the state completed), and Virginia (1.471M acres). Wetland density (wetland acres/unit area) was highest in states dominated by the coastal plain - Delaware had the highest density of wetland with 21 percent of the state covered by wetland, followed closely by New Jersey with 20 percent. Virginia and Maryland, the Chesapeake Bay states, had the most tidal wetland acreage, followed by New Jersey. Estuarine emergent wetlands (salt and brackish marshes) were the dominant tidal wetland type across the region, whereas forested wetlands dominated freshwater environments.

In addition to creating NWI maps and geospatial data, the Region's NWI Program has produced a variety of other products including multi-state wetland trends analysis reports, inventory of wetland change reports, watershed-based wetland characterizations and preliminary functional assessments, and inventories of potential wetland restoration sites. These products plus the digital geospatial data and accompanying status reports have greatly increased our knowledge of the extent, distribution, and diversity of wetlands, their status and trends, wetland functions, and opportunities for their restoration. As such, the NWI has provided vital information to various Service programs, other federal agencies, state agencies, and others that has been used to help protect, conserve, and restore our nation's wetlands.

References

Bailey, R.G. 1994. Ecoregions of the United States. U.S.D.A. Forest Service, Washington, DC. Map (scale 1:7,500,000). Revised. http://www.fs.fed.us/rm/ecoregions/products/map-ecoregions-united-states/

Ciminelli, J. and J. Scrivani. 2007. Virginia Conservation Lands Needs Assessment: Virginia Watershed Integrity Model. Virginia Department of Conservation and Recreation-Division of Natural Heritage, Virginia Department of Forestry, Virginia Commonwealth University-Center for Environmental Studies, and Virginia Department of Environmental Quality-Coastal Zone Management Program. http://www.dcr.virginia.gov/natural_heritage/vclnawater.shtml

Cowardin, L.M., V. Carter, F.C. Golet, and E.T. LaRoe. 1979. Classification of Wetlands and Deepwater Habitats of the United States. U.S. Fish and Wildlife Service, Washington, DC. FWS-OBS/79-61. http://library.fws.gov/FWS-OBS/79_31.pdf

Dahl, T.E. 2006. Status and Trends of Wetlands in the Conterminous United States 1998 to 2004. U.S. Department of the Interior, Fish and Wildlife Service, Washington, DC. http://www.fws.gov/wetlands/_documents/gSandT/NationalReports/StatusTrendsWetlandsConterminousUS1998to2004.pdf

FGDC Wetlands Subcommittee. 2009. Wetland Mapping Standard. Federal Geographic Data Committee Document Number FGDC-STD-015-2009. http://www.fws.gov/wetlands/_documents/gNSDI/FGDCWetlandsMappingStandard.pdf

Frayer, W.E., T.J. Monahan, D.C. Bowden, and F.A. Graybill. 1983. Status and Trends of Wetlands and Deepwater Habitats in the Conterminous United States 1950's to 1970's. Department of Forest and Wood Sciences, Colorado State University, Ft. Collins, CO.

Tiner, R.W. (ed.). 2009. Status Report for the National Wetlands Inventory Program: 2009. U.S. Fish and Wildlife Service, Division of Habitat and Resource Conservation, Branch of Resource and Mapping Support, Washington, DC. http://www.fws.gov/wetlands/_documents/gOther/StatusReportNWIProgram2009.pdf

Tiner, R.W. 2005. In Search of Swampland: A Wetland Sourcebook and Field Guide. Revised and Expanded 2nd Edition. Rutgers University Press, New Brunswick, NJ.

Tiner, R.W. 2003a. Dichotomous Keys and Mapping Codes for Wetland Landscape Position, Landform, Water Flow Path, and Waterbody Type Descriptors. U.S. Fish and Wildlife Service, Northeast Region, Hadley, MA. http://library.fws.gov/Wetlands/dichotomouskeys0903.pdf

Tiner, R.W. 2003b. Correlating Enhanced National Wetlands Inventory Data With Wetland Functions for Watershed Assessments: A Rationale for Northeastern U.S. Wetlands. U.S. Fish and Wildlife Service, Northeast Region, Hadley, MA. http://library.fws.gov/Wetlands/corelate_wetlandsNE.pdf

Tiner, R.W. 2004. Remotely-sensed indicators for monitoring the general condition of "natural habitat" in watersheds: an application for Delaware's Nanticoke River watershed. Ecological Indicators 4: 227-243. http://wetlands.fws.gov/Pubs_Reports/EcologicalIndicatorsTiner.pdf

Tiner, R.W. 1999. Wetland Indicators. A Guide to Wetland Identification, Delineation, Classification, and Mapping. Lewis Publishers, CRC Press, Boca Raton, FL.

Tiner, R.W. 1984. Wetlands of the United States: Current Status and Recent Trends. U.S. Department of the Interior, Fish and Wildlife Service, Washington, DC. http://www.fws.gov/wetlands/_documents/gSandT/NationalReports/WetlandsUSCurrentStatusRecentTrends1984.pdf

Tiner, R.W. and H.C. Bergquist. 2007. The Hackensack River Watershed, New Jersey/New York Wetland Characterization, Preliminary Assessment of Wetland Functions, and Remotely-sensed Assessment of Natural Habitat Integrity. U.S. Fish and Wildlife Service, National Wetlands Inventory, Ecological Services, Region 5, Hadley, MA. http://library.fws.gov/Wetlands/HackensackRiverWatershed07.pdf

Tiner, R.W., Jr., and J.T. Finn. 1986. Status and Recent Trends of Wetlands in Five Mid-Atlantic States: Delaware, Maryland, Pennsylvania, Virginia, and West Virginia. U.S. Fish and Wildlife Service, Region 5, National Wetlands Inventory Project, Newton Corner, MA and U.S. Environmental Protection Agency, Region III, Philadelphia, PA. Cooperative publication. http://www.fws.gov/wetlands/_documents/gSandT/StateRegionalReports/StatusRecentTrendsWetlandsFiveMidAtlanticStates.pdf

Vance, L.K., K. Newlon, J. Clarke, and D.M. Stagliano. 2009. Assessment of Red Rock River Subbasin and Wetlands of the Centennial Valley. Report to the Bureau of Land Management, Montana/Dakotas State Offices. Montana Natural Heritage Program, Helena, MT. http://mtnhp.org/Reports/BLM_2009.pdf

APPENDIX A. LIST OF PRIMARY CONTRIBUTORS TO THE NWI FOR THE NORTHEAST

The following agencies have contributed to the Region's NWI Program by providing funding to support wetland mapping or other products or have contributed to the NWI Program by performing photointerpretation/image analysis or distributing NWI maps.

Federal Agencies

Army Corps of Engineers, New England, New York, Philadelphia, and Buffalo Districts
Natural Resource Conservation Service, Maine
Fish and Wildlife Service, Region 5 Refuges Program
Environmental Protection Agency, Regions 1, 2, and 3
Department of Defense

State Agencies

Connecticut Department of Environmental Protection
Delaware Department of Natural Resources and Environmental Control
Maine Geological Survey*
Maine Office of GIS
Maine State Planning Office
Maine Land Use Regulation Commission
Maryland Department of Natural Resources
Maryland Geological Survey*
Massachusetts Executive Office of Environmental Affairs
New Hampshire Office of State Planning*
New Jersey Department of Environmental Protection
New York Department of Environmental Conservation
Pennsylvania Department of Environmental Protection
Rhode Island Department of Environmental Management
Vermont Department of Environmental Conservation*
Virginia Department of Conservation and Recreation
West Virginia Division of Natural Resources

Local Governments

Kent County Conservation District (DE)
New York City Department of Environmental Protection (NY)
Suffolk County (NY)
Tompkins County (NY)
Ulster County (NY)

Universities

Cornell University*
University of Massachusetts*#
Virginia Polytechnic Institute and State University (Virginia Tech) #

*Map distribution centers

#Photointerpretation, image analysis, and data compilation

APPENDIX B. OVERVIEW OF THE SERVICE'S WETLAND CLASSIFICATION SYSTEM

The following section represents a simplified overview of the Service's wetland classification system. Consequently, some of the more technical points have been omitted from this discussion. When actually classifying a wetland, the reader is advised to refer to the official classification document (Cowardin et al. 1979; http://library.fws.gov/FWS-OBS/79_31.pdf) and should not rely solely on this overview.

Overview of the Service's Wetland Classification System

The Service's wetland classification system is hierarchial or vertical in nature proceeding from general to specific. In this approach, wetlands are first defined at a rather broad level the SYSTEM. The term SYSTEM represents "a complex of wetlands and deepwater habitats that share the influence of similar hydrologic, geomorphologic, chemical, or biological factors." Five systems are defined: Marine, Estuarine, Riverine, Lacustrine, and Palustrine. The Marine System generally consists of the open ocean and its associated high energy coastline, while the Estuarine System encompasses salt and brackish marshes, nonvegetated tidal shores, and brackish waters of coastal rivers and embayments. Freshwater wetlands and deepwater habitats fall into one of the other three systems: Riverine (rivers and streams), Lacustrine (lakes, reservoirs and large ponds), or Palustrine (e.g., marshes, bogs, swamps and small shallow ponds). Thus, at the most general level, wetlands can be defined as either Marine, Estuarine, Riverine, Lacustrine or Palustrine.

Each system, with the exception of the Palustrine, is further subdivided into SUBSYSTEMS. The Marine and Estuarine Systems both have the same two subsystems, which are defined by tidal water levels: (1) Subtidal continuously submerged areas and (2) Intertidal areas alternately flooded by tides and exposed to air. Similarly, the Lacustrine System is separated into two systems based on water depth: (1) Littoral wetlands extending from the lake shore to a depth of 6.6 feet (2 m) below low water or to the extent of nonpersistent emergents (e.g., arrowheads, pickerelweed, or spatterdock) if they grow beyond that depth, and (2) Limnetic deepwater habitats lying beyond the 6.6 feet (2 m) at low water. By contrast, the Riverine System is further defined by four subsystems that represent different reaches of a flowing freshwater or lotic system: (1) Tidal water levels subject to tidal fluctuations for at least part of the growing season, (2) Lower Perennial permanent, flowing waters with a well developed floodplain, (3) Upper Perennial permanent, flowing water with very little or no floodplain development, and (4) Intermittent channel containing nontidal flowing water for only part of the year.

The next level - CLASS - describes the general appearance of the wetland or deepwater habitat in terms of the dominant vegetative life form or the nature and composition of the substrate, where vegetative cover is less than 30% (Table B-1). Of the 11 classes, five refer to areas where vegetation covers 30% or more of the surface: Aquatic Bed, Moss Lichen Wetland, Emergent Wetland, Scrub Shrub Wetland and Forested Wetland. The remaining six classes represent areas generally lacking vegetation, where the composition of the substrate and degree of flooding distinguish classes: Rock Bottom, Unconsolidated Bottom, Reef (sedentary invertebrate colony), Streambed, Rocky Shore, and Unconsolidated Shore. Permanently flooded nonvegetated areas are classified as either Rock Bottom or Unconsolidated Bottom, while exposed areas are typed as Streambed, Rocky Shore, or Unconsolidated Shore. Invertebrate reefs are found in both permanently flooded and exposed areas.

Each class is further divided into SUBCLASSES to better define the type of substrate in nonvegetated areas (e.g., bedrock, rubble, cobble gravel, mud, sand, and organic) or the type of dominant vegetation (e.g., persistent or nonpersistent emergents, moss, lichen, or broad leaved deciduous, needle leaved deciduous, broad-leaved evergreen, needle leaved evergreen and dead woody plants). Below the subclass level, DOMINANCE TYPE can be applied to specify the predominant plant or animal in the wetland community.

To allow better description of a given wetland or deepwater habitat in regard to hydrologic, chemical and soil characteristics and to human impacts, the classification system contains four types of specific modifiers: (1) Water Regime, (2) Water Chemistry, (3) Soil, and (4) Special. These modifiers may be applied to class and lower levels of the classification hierarchy.

Water regime modifiers describe flooding or soil saturation conditions and are divided into two main groups: tidal and nontidal. Tidal water regimes are used where water level fluctuations are largely driven by oceanic tides. Tidal regimes can be subdivided into two general categories, one for salt and brackish water tidal areas and another for freshwater tidal areas. This distinction is needed because of the special importance of seasonal river overflow and ground water inflows in freshwater tidal areas. By contrast, nontidal modifiers define conditions where surface water runoff, ground water discharge, and/or wind effects (i.e., lake seiches) cause water level changes. Both tidal and nontidal water regime modifiers are presented and briefly defined in Table B-2.

Water chemistry modifiers are divided into two categories which describe the water's salinity or hydrogen ion concentration (pH): (1) salinity modifiers and (2) pH modifiers. Like water regimes, salinity modifiers have been further subdivided into two groups: halinity modifiers for tidal areas and salinity modifiers for nontidal areas. Estuarine and marine waters are dominated by sodium chloride, which is gradually diluted by fresh water as one moves upstream in coastal rivers. On the other hand, the salinity of inland waters is dominated by four major cations (i.e., calcium, magnesium, sodium, and potassium) and three major anions (i.e., carbonate, sulfate, and chloride). Interactions between precipitation, surface runoff, ground water flow, evaporation, and sometimes plant evapotranspiration form inland salts which are most common in arid and semiarid regions of the country. Table B-3 shows ranges of halinity and salinity modifiers which are a modification of the Venice System (Remane and Schlieper 1971). The other set of water chemistry modifiers are pH modifiers for identifying acid (pH<5.5), circumneutral (5.5 7.4) and alkaline (pH>7.4) waters. Some studies have shown a good correlation between plant distribution and pH levels (Sjors 1950; Jeglum 1971). Moreover, pH can be used to distinguish between mineral rich (e.g., fens) and mineral poor wetlands (e.g., bogs).

The third group of modifiers soil modifiers are presented because the nature of the soil exerts strong influences on plant growth and reproduction as well as on the animals living in it. Two soil modifiers are given: (1) mineral and (2) organic. In general, if a soil has 20% or more organic matter by weight in the upper 16 inches, it is considered an organic soil, whereas if it has less than this amount, it is a mineral soil. For specific definitions, please refer to Appendix D of the Service's classification system (Cowardin et al. 1979) or to Soil Taxonomy (Soil Survey Staff 1975).

The final set of modifiers special modifiers were established to describe the activities of people or beaver affecting wetlands and deepwater habitats. These modifiers include: excavated, impounded (i.e., to obstruct outflow of water), diked (i.e., to obstruct inflow of water), partly drained, farmed, and artificial (i.e., materials deposited to create or modify a wetland or deepwater habitat).

References

Cowardin, L.M., V. Carter, F.C. Golet and E.T. LaRoe. 1979. Classification of Wetlands and Deepwater Habitats of the United States. U.S. Fish and Wildlife Service, Washington, DC. FWS/OBS 79/31. 103 pp.

Jeglum, J.K. 1971. Plant indicators of pH and water level in peat lands at Candle Lake, Saskatchewan. Can. J. Bot. 49: 1661 1676.

Remane, A. and C. Schlieper. 1971. Biology of Brackish Water. Wiley Interscience Division, John Wiley & Sons, New York. 372 pp.

Sjors, H. 1950. On the relation between vegetation and electro¬lytes in north Swedish mire waters. Oikos 2: 241 258.

Soil Survey Staff. 1975. Soil Taxonomy. Department of Agriculture, Soil Conservation Service, Washington, DC. Agriculture Handbook No. 436. 754 pp.

Table B-1. Classes and subclasses of wetlands and deepwater habitats (Cowardin et al. 1979).

Class	Brief Description	Subclasses
Rock Bottom	Generally permanently flooded areas with bottom substrates consisting of at least 75% stones and boulders and less than 30% vegetative cover.	Bedrock; Rubble
Unconsolidated Bottom	Generally permanently flooded areas with bottom substrates consisting of at least 25% particles smaller than stones and less than 30% vegetative cover.	Cobble-gravel; Sand; Mud; Organic
Aquatic Bed	Generally permanently flooded areas vegetated by plants growing principally on or below the water surface line.	Algal; Aquatic Moss; Rooted Vascular; Floating Vascular
Reef	Ridge-like or mound-like structures formed by the colonization and growth of sedentary invertebrates.	Coral; Mollusk; Worm
Streambed	Channel whose bottom is completely dewatered at low water periods.	Bedrock; Rubble; Cobble-gravel; Sand; Mud; Organic; Vegetated (pioneer)
Rocky Shore	Wetlands characterized by bedrock, stones or boulders with areal coverage of 75% or more and with less than 30% coverage by vegetation.	Bedrock; Rubble
Unconsolidated Shore	Wetlands having unconsolidated substrates with less than 75% coverage by stone, boulders and bedrock and less than 30% vegetative cover, except by pioneer plants.	Cobble-gravel; Sand; Mud; Organic; Vegetated (pioneer)
Moss-Lichen Wetland	Wetlands dominated by mosses or lichens where other plants have less than 30% coverage.	Moss; Lichen
Emergent Wetland	Wetlands dominated by erect, rooted, herbaceous hydrophytes.	Persistent; Nonpersistent
Scrub-Shrub Wetland	Wetlands dominated by woody vegetation less than 20 feet (6 m) tall.	Broad-leaved Deciduous; Needle-leaved Deciduous; Needle-leaved Evergreen; Dead
Forested Wetland	Wetlands dominated by woody vegetation 20 feet (6 m) or taller.	Broad-leaved Deciduous; Needle-leaved Deciduous; Broad-leaved Evergreen; Needle-leaved Evergreen; Dead

Table B-2. Water regime modifiers, both tidal and nontidal groups (Cowardin et al. 1979).

Group	Type of Water	Water Regime	Definition
Tidal	Saltwater and brackish areas	Subtidal	Permanently flooded tidal waters
		Irregularly exposed	Exposed less often than daily by tides
		Regularly flooded	Daily tidal flooding and exposure to air
		Irregularly flooded	Flooded less often than daily and typically exposed to air
	Freshwater	Permanently flooded-tidal	Permanently flooded by tides and river or exposed irregularly by tides
		Semipermanently flooded-tidal	Flooded for most of the growing season by river overflow but with tidal fluctuation in water levels
		Regularly flooded	Daily tidal flooding and exposure to air
		Seasonally flooded-tidal	Flooded irregularly by tides and seasonally by river overflow
		Temporarily flooded-tidal	Flooded irregularly by tides and for brief periods during growing season by river overflow
Nontidal	Inland freshwater and saline areas	Permanently flooded	Flooded throughout the year in all years
		Intermittently exposed	Flooded year-round except during extreme droughts
		Semipermanently flooded	Flooded throughout the growing season in most years
		Seasonally flooded	Flooded for extended periods in growing season, but surface water is usually absent by end of growing season
		Saturated	Surface water is seldom present, but substrate is saturated to the surface for most of the season
		Temporarily flooded	Flooded for only brief periods during growing season, with water table usually well below the soil surface for most of the season

Table B-2. Water regime modifiers, both tidal and nontidal groups (Cowardin et al. 1979). continued

Group	Type of Water	Water Regime	Definition
Nontidal	Inland freshwater and saline areas	Intermittently flooded	Substrate is usually exposed and only flooded for variable periods without detectable seasonal periodicity (not always wetland; may be upland in some situations)
		Artificially flooded	Duration and amount of flooding is controlled by means of pumps or siphons in combination with dikes or dams

Table B-3. Salinity modifiers for coastal and inland areas (Cowardin et al. 1979).

Coastal Modifiers[5]	Inland Modifiers[6]	Salinity (l)	Approximate Specific Conductance (Mhos at 25° C)
Hyperhaline	Hypersaline	> 40	> 60,000
Euhaline	Eusaline	30-40	45,000-60,000
Mixohaline (Brackish)	Mixosaline[7]	0.5-30	800-45,000
Polyhaline	Polysaline	18-30	30,000-45,000
Mesohaline	Mesosaline	5-18	8,000-30,000
Oligohaline	Oligosaline	0.5-5	800-8,000
Fresh	Fresh	< 0.5	< 800

---

[5] Coastal modifiers are employed in the Marine and Estuarine Systems.

[6] Inland modifiers are employed in the Riverine, Lacustrine and Palustrine Systems.

[7] The term "brackish" should not be used for inland wetlands or deepwater habitats.

APPENDIX C. LIST OF REGIONAL NWI PUBLICATIONS

(Note: Publications are listed by major topic.)

The following is a list of publications produced by the U.S. Fish and Wildlife Service, Northeast Region. Publications are arranged by general topics. Some of these reports are online publications posted on the NWI website (http:// wetlands.fws.gov), click on "documents search engine" then type in title of the publication in the "key words" block. Some are online documents at the Service's Conservation Library and direct links are given. All publications with numbers in the margin can be obtained free of charge from: U.S, Fish and Wildlife Service, Ecological Services, 300 Westgate Center Drive, Hadley, MA 01035-9589. Your request can be mailed in or emailed to ralph_tiner@fws.gov. On email, please note "publication order" in the subject block.

WETLAND DEFINITION, CLASSIFICATION, AND BASIC CONCEPTS

101   *"Wetlands are Ecotones - Reality or Myth?"*

102   *"How wet is a wetland?"*

103   *"The concept of a hydrophyte for wetland identification" (BioScience)*

104   *"Classification of wetland ecosystems"*

195   *"A Clarification of the U.S. Fish and Wildlife Service's Wetland Definition"*

        Dichotomous Keys and Mapping Codes for Wetland Landscape Position, Landform, Water Flow Path, and Waterbody Type Descriptors by R. Tiner. September 2003.
        http://library.fws.gov/Wetlands/dichotomouskeys0903.pdf

167   *"Technical Aspects of Wetlands: Wetland Definitions and Classifications in the United States"* by R. Tiner. 1997.

        Geographically Isolated Wetlands: A Preliminary Assessment of Their Characteristics and Status in Selected Areas of the United States 2002. U.S. Fish and Wildlife Service, Northeast Region, Hadley, MA. http://library.fws.gov/Wetlands/isolated.pdf

WETLAND AND RIPARIAN MAPPING

105   *"The National Wetlands Inventory - The First Ten Years"*

106   *"Creating a National Georeferenced Wetland Database for Managing Wetlands in the United States"*

107   *"Use of high-altitude aerial photography for inventorying forested wetlands in the United States"*

108   *NWI Maps Made Easy: A User's Guide to National Wetlands Inventory Maps of the Northeast Region* by G.S. Smith. 1991.

111   *Comparison of Four Scales of Color Infrared Photography for Wetland Mapping in Maryland* by R.W. Tiner and G.S. Smith. 1992. U.S. Fish and Wildlife Service, Region 5, Newton Corner, MA. National Wetlands Inventory Report. R5-92/03. 15 pp. plus tables.

        An Investigation and Verification of Draft NWI Maps for Cape May County, New Jersey by U.S. Fish and Wildlife Service, New Jersey Field Office. 1992. Available from: New Jersey Field Office, U.S. Fish and Wildlife Service, 927 N. Main Street (Bldg. D-1), Pleasantville, NJ 08232.

158   *Map Accuracy of National Wetlands Inventory Maps for Areas Subject to Maine Land Use Regulation Commission Jurisdiction* by C. Nichols. 1994.

162   *Assessment of Remote Sensing/GIS Technologies to Improve National Wetlands Inventory Maps* by B. Wilen and G. Smith. 1996. Proceedings: Sixth Biennial Forest Service Remote Sensing Applications Conference, Denver, CO.

164   "Some Uses of National Wetlands Inventory Maps and Digital Map Data in the Northeast".

166   "NWI Maps: What They Tell Us".

170   "Adapting the NWI for Preliminary Assessment of Wetland Functions", R.W. Tiner. 1997. *In*: The Future of Wetland Assessment: Applying Science through the Hydrogeomorphic Assessment Approach and Other Approaches. The Association of State Wetland Managers Institute for Wetland Science and Public Policy.

171   "NWI Maps--Basic Information on the Nation's Wetlands", Ralph Tiner. *In*: BioScience. May 1997.

172   "Piloting a More Descriptive NWI", Ralph Tiner. In: National Wetlands Newsletter, Vol. 19(5). September-October 1997.

WETLAND IDENTIFICATION - FIELD GUIDES

Field Guide to Nontidal Wetland Identification by R.W. Tiner, Jr. 1988. Maryland Department of Natural Resources and U.S. Fish and Wildlife Service. Cooperative publication. 283 pp. + 198 color plates. Full color reproductions are available for purchase from:. http://www.wetlanded.com

WETLAND DELINEATION - MANUALS/ARTICLES

189   *An Overview of Wetland Identification and Delineation Techniques, with Recommendations for Improvement* by Ralph W. Tiner. 2000. Wetland Journal, Volume 12, Number 1, Winter 2000. P.O. Box P, 201 Boundary Lane, St. Michaels, Maryland 21663, (410) 745-9620

       "The Primary Indicators Method - A Practical Approach to Wetland Recognition and Delineation in the United States" (Wetlands) http://library.fws.gov/Wetlands/TINER_WETLANDS13.pdf

113   "Using Plants as Indicators of Wetland" (Proceedings of The Academy of Natural Sciences of Philadelphia)

114   "Wetland boundary delineation"

115   "Wetland delineation 1991"

116   "Technical issues regarding wetland delineation"

161   "Practical Considerations for Wetland Identification and Boundary Delineation"

HYDRIC SOILS

Hydric Soils of New England by R.W. Tiner, Jr. and P.L.M. Veneman. Revised edition June 1995. University of Massachusetts Cooperative Extension, Bulletin C-183R, Amherst, MA. Available from: University of Massachusetts Extension, Bulletin Center, Cottage A, Thatcher Way, Amherst, MA 01003. http://www.umassextension.org/Merchant2/merchant.mv

WETLAND PLANT LISTS/HYDROPHYTES

Lists of Potential Hydrophytes for the United States: A Regional Review and Their Use in Wetland Identification by R.W. Tiner. 2006. WETLANDS 26(2):624-634. Available online at: http://www.fws.gov/wetlands/ (use documents search engine).

WETLAND PLANT - SOIL CORRELATION STUDIES

Soil-Vegetation Correlations in the Connecticut River Floodplain of Western Massachusetts by Peter Veneman and Ralph Tiner, September 1990, U.S Fish and Wildlife Service, Washington D.C. Biological Report 90(6). http://library.fws.gov/BiologicalReports/BR_90_6.pdf

STATE WETLAND REPORTS

Wetlands of New Jersey by R.W. Tiner, Jr. 1985. U.S. Fish and Wildlife Service, Region 5, National Wetlands Inventory Project, Newton Corner, MA. http://library.fws.gov/Wetlands/NJ_wetlands85.pdf

Wetlands of Delaware by R.W. Tiner, Jr. 1985. U.S. Fish and Wildlife Service, Region 5, National Wetlands Inventory Project, Hadley, MA and Delaware Department of Natural Resources and Environmental Control, Wetlands Section, Dover, DE. Cooperative publication.

Wetlands of Rhode Island by R.W. Tiner. 1989. U.S. Fish and Wildlife Service, Region 5, National Wetlands Inventory Project, Newton Corner, MA. http://library.fws.gov/Wetlands/RI_wetlands89.pdf

Wetlands of Connecticut by K. Metzler and R.W. Tiner. 1991. Connecticut Department of Environmental Protection, Hartford, CT. http://www.fws.gov/wetlands/_documents/gOther/WetlandsConnecticut.pdf

Wetlands of Maryland by R.W. Tiner and D.G. Burke. 1995. U.S. Fish and Wildlife Service, Ecological Services, Region 5, Hadley, MA and Maryland Department of Natural Resources, Annapolis, MD. Cooperative publication. http://library.fws.gov/Wetlands/MD_wetlands85.pdf

West Virginia's Wetlands. Uncommon, Valuable Wildlands by R.W. Tiner. 1996. U.S. Fish and Wildlife Service, Ecological Services, Northeast Region, Hadley, MA. http://www.fws.gov/wetlands/_documents/gOther/WestVirginiasWetlandsUncommonValuableWildlands.pdf

Current Status of West Virginia's Wetlands by R.W. Tiner. 1996. U.S. Fish and Wildlife Service, Hadley, MA. http://www.fws.gov/wetlands/_documents/gOther/CurrentStatusWestVirginiasWetlands.pdf

Maine Wetlands and Waters by R.W. Tiner. 2007. U.S. Fish and Wildlife Service, National Wetlands Inventory Program, Northeast Region, Hadley, MA. Available online at: http://library.fws.gov/Wetlands/maine07.pdf

New Hampshire Wetlands and Waters by R.W. Tiner. 2007. U.S. Fish and Wildlife Service, National Wetlands Inventory Program, Northeast Region, Hadley, MA. Available online at: http://library.fws.gov/Wetlands/NH07.pdf

WETLAND STATUS AND TREND REPORTS (estimates of wetland change)

123   *Recent Changes in Estuarine Wetlands of the Conterminous United States* by R.W. Tiner. 1991. Reprinted from "Coastal Wetlands", Coastal Zone '91 Conference-ASCE, Long Beach, CA. 10 pp.

        Wetlands of the United States: Current Status and Recent Trends by R.W. Tiner, Jr. 1984. U.S. Fish and Wildlife Service, National Wetlands Inventory. http://www.fws.gov/wetlands/_documents/gSandT/NationalReports/WetlandsUSCurrentStatusRecentTrends1984.pdf

124   *Status and Recent Trends of Wetlands in Five Mid-Atlantic States: Delaware, Maryland, Pennsylvania, Virginia, and West Virginia* by R.W. Tiner, Jr. and J.T. Finn. 1986. http://www.fws.gov/wetlands/_documents/gSandT/StateRegionalReports/StatusRecentTrendsWetlandsFiveMidAtlanticStates.pdf

INVENTORIES OF WETLAND CHANGE REPORTS

125   *Current Status and Recent Trends in Wetlands in Central Connecticut* by R.W. Tiner, J. Stone, and J. Gookin. 1989.

126   *Recent Wetland Trends in Southeastern Massachusetts* by R.W. Tiner, Jr. and W. Zinni, Jr. 1988.

127   *Pennsylvania's Wetlands: Current Status and Recent Trends* by R.W. Tiner. 1990.

128   *Current Status and Recent Trends in Wetlands of the Lake Erie and Delaware Estuary Coastal Zones of Pennsylvania (1986-1989)* by G.S. Smith and R.W. Tiner. 1992.

129   *Recent Wetland Trends in Anne Arundel County, Maryland (1981-82 to 1988-90)* by R.W. Tiner and D.B. Foulis. 1992.

130   *Wetland Trends in Prince Georges County, Maryland From 1981 to 1988-89* by R.W. Tiner and D.B. Foulis. 1992.

131   *Wetland Status and Trends for the Pleasant Valley Quadrangle, Dutchess County, New York (1958-1988)* by Ralph W. Tiner and Glenn S. Smith. 1993.

132   "Agricultural impacts on wetlands in the northeastern United States" by Ralph W. Tiner, Jr. 1988.

133   *Status and Trends of Wetlands in Cape May County, New Jersey and Vicinity (1977 to 1991)* by G.S. Smith and R.W. Tiner. 1993.

134   *Wetland Status and Trends in Selected Areas of Maryland's Piedmont Region (1980-81 to 1988-89)* by R.W. Tiner and D.B. Foulis. 1993.

135   *Wetland Status and Trends in Selected Areas of Maryland's Fall Zone (1981-82 to 1988-89)* by R.W. Tiner and D.B. Foulis. 1993.

136   *Wetland Trends in Selected Areas of the Western Shore Region of Maryland (1981 to 1988)* by R.W. Tiner and D.B. Foulis. 1993.

137   *Wetland Trends for the North East Quadrangle in Maryland (1981 to 1988)* by R.W. Tiner and D.B. Foulis. 1993.

138   *Wetland Trends for the Kent Island and Queenstown Quadrangles in Eastern Maryland (1982 to 1989)* by R.W. Tiner and D.B. Foulis. 1993.

139   *Wetland Trends for the DuBois and Falls Creek Quadrangles in Pennsylvania (1983 to 1988)* by R.W. Tiner and D.B. Foulis. 1993.

140   *Wetland Trends in the Williamsport Area of Pennsylvania (1977 to 1988/90)* by R.W. Tiner and D.B. Foulis. 1993.

141   *Wetland Trends for the Hazelton Quadrangle in Pennsylvania (1981 to 1987)* by R.W. Tiner and D.B. Foulis. 1993.

142   *Wetland Trends in Selected Areas of the Greater Harrisburg Region of Pennsylvania (1983-84 to 1987-88)* by R.W. Tiner and D.B. Foulis. 1993.

143   *Wetland Trends for Selected Areas of the Northeast Glaciated Region of Pennsylvania (1981-82 to 1987-88)* by R.W. Tiner, D.B. Foulis, and T.W. Nuerminger. 1994.

144   *Wetland Trends for Selected Areas of Dorchester County, Maryland and Vicinity (1981-82 to 1988-89)* by R.W. Tiner and D.B. Foulis. 1994.

144a   *Wetland Trends in Dorchester County, Maryland (1981-82 to 1988-89)* by D.B. Foulis, T.W. Nuerminger, and R.W. Tiner. 1995.

145   *Wetland Trends for Selected Areas of the Lower Eastern Shore of the Delmarva Peninsula (1982 to 1988-89)* by R.W. Tiner and D.B. Foulis. 1994.

146   *Wetland Trends in Selected Areas of the Norfolk/Hampton Region of Virginia (1982 to 1989-90)* by R.W. Tiner and D.B. Foulis. 1994.

147   *Wetland Trends for Selected Areas in Northern Virginia (1980-81 to 1988/91)* by R.W. Tiner and D.B. Foulis. 1994.

148   *Wetland Trends for Selected Areas of the Chickahominy River Watershed of Virginia (1982/84 to 1989-90)* by R.W. Tiner and D.B. Foulis. 1994.

       Recent Wetland Status and Trends in the Chesapeake Watershed (1982 to 1989): Technical Report by R.W. Tiner, I. Kenenski, T. Nuerminger, D.B. Foulis, J. Eaton, G.S. Smith, and W.E. Frayer. 1994. Chesapeake Bay Program, Annapolis, MD. http://www.fws.gov/wetlands/_documents/gSandT/StateRegionalReports/RecentWetlandStatusTrendsChesapeakeWatershed1982to1989.pdf

149   *Recent Wetland Status and Trends in the Chesapeake Watershed (1982 to 1989): Executive Summary Report* by R.W. Tiner. 1994.

150   *Wetland Trends for Selected Areas of the Casco Bay Estuary of the Gulf of Maine (1974-77 to 1984-87)* by D.B. Foulis and R.W. Tiner. 1994.

151   *Wetland Trends for Selected Areas of the Cobscook Bay/St. Croix River Estuary of the Gulf of Maine (1975/77 to 1983-85)* by D.B. Foulis and R.W. Tiner. 1994.

152   *Wetland Trends for Selected Areas of the Coast of Massachusetts, from Plum Island to Scituate (1977 to 1985-86)* by D.B. Foulis and R.W. Tiner. 1994.

153   *Wetland Trends for Selected Areas of the Gulf of Maine, from York, Maine to Rowley, Massachusetts (1977 to 1985-86)* by D.B. Foulis, J.A. Eaton, and R.W. Tiner. 1994.

154   *Wetland Status and Trends in Charles County, Maryland (1981 to 1988-89)* by D.B. Foulis and R.W. Tiner. 1994.

155   *Wetland Status and Trends in St. Marys County, Maryland (1981-82 to 1988-89)* by D.B. Foulis and R.W. Tiner. 1994.

156   *Wetland Status and Trends in Calvert County, Maryland (1981-82 to 1988-89)* by D.B. Foulis and R.W. Tiner. 1994.

168   *New York Tidal Wetland Trends: Pilot Study in Shinnecock Bay Estuary and Recommendations for Statewide Analysis* by R.W. Tiner. 1987.

173   *Current Status of West Virginia's Wetlands: Results of the National Wetlands Inventory* by R.W. Tiner. 1996.

       Chesapeake Bay Wetlands: The Vital Link Between the Watershed and the Bay. 14 pp. booklet. Available from: U.S. Fish and Wildlife Service, Chesapeake Bay Field Office, 177 Admiral Cochrane Drive, Annapolis, MD 21401; (410) 573-4583.

177   *Wetland Status and Recent Trends for the Neponset Watershed, Massachusetts (1977-1991)* by R.W. Tiner, D.B. Foulis, C. Nichols, S. Schaller, D. Petersen, K. Andersen, and John Swords. 1998.

       Delaware's Wetlands: Status and Recent Trends by R.W. Tiner. June 2001. http://www.fws.gov/wetlands/_documents/gSandT/StateRegionalReports/DelawaresWetlandsStatusRecentTrends.pdf

       Wetland Status and Trends for the Hackensack Meadowlands: An Assessment Report from the National Wetlands Inventory Program by R.W. Tiner, J.Q. Swords, and B.J. McClain. 2002. http://library.fws.gov/wetlands/hackensack.pdf.

       Coastal Wetland Trends in the Narragansett Bay Estuary During the 20th Century by R.W. Tiner, I.J. Huber, T. Nuerminger, and A.L. Mandeville. 2004. http://library.fws.gov/Wetlands/narragansett04.pdf

       Recent Wetland Trends in Southeastern Virginia: 1994-2000. by R.W. Tiner, J.Q. Swords, and H.C. Bergquist. 2005. http://library.fws.gov/Wetlands/sevirginia05.pdf

100 Years of Estuarine Marsh Trends (1893 to 1995): Boston Harbor, Cape Cod, Nantucket, Martha's Vineyard, and the Elizabeth Islands by B.K. Carlisle, R.W. Tiner, M. Carullo, I. J. Huber, T. Nuerminger, C. Polzen, and M. Shaffer. 2006. http://www.mass.gov/czm/estuarine_marsh_ trend1.htm

Mid-Atlantic Wetlands: A Disappearing Natural Treasure by R.W. Tiner. 1987. http://library.fws.gov/Wetlands/midatlantic.pdf

Salt Marsh Trends in Selected Estuaries in Southwestern Connecticut by R.W. Tiner and others. 2006. http://library.fws.gov/wetlands/saltmarsh_ct06.pdf

INVENTORY REPORTS/ARTICLES

182   *Wetland Trends in the Croton Watershed, New York (1968-1994)* by R. Tiner, J. Swords, and S. Schaller. 1999.

183   *Wetland Trends in Delaware: 1981/2 to 1992* by R. Tiner, J. Swords, and S. Schaller. 1999.

192   *The Peconic Watershed: Recent Trends in Wetlands and their Buffers*. R.W. Tiner and others. 2000.

201   *Geographically Isolated Wetlands of the United States* by R.W. Tiner, U. S. Fish and Wildlife Service. Also in Wetlands, Vol 23, No.3, Sept. 2003, pp 494-516, The Society of Wetland Scientists

202   *Estimated Extent of Geographically Isolated Wetlands in Selected Areas of the United States* by Ralph Tiner, U.S. Fish and Wildlife Service. In Wetlands, Vol 23, No.3, Sept. 2003, pp 636-652, The Society of Wetland Scientists

OTHER REGIONAL WETLAND INVENTORY REPORTS/ARTICLES

117   *Preliminary NWI Wetland Acreage Reports for Massachusetts (1992) and Vermont (1987)* by R. W. Tiner, U.S. Fish and Wildlife Service, NWI Project, Newton Corner, MA

118   *Wetlands Inventory of the FAA Technical Center, Atlantic City International Airport, New Jersey* by Ralph W. Tiner and Glenn S. Smith. 1993.

119   "Vascular plant communities in wetlands of Pennsylvania"

120   "Current status and recent trends in Pennsylvania's wetlands"

121   "Wetlands of the Delaware River Basin"

       The Wetlands of Acadia National Park and Vicinity. A joint publication of the Department of Wildlife Ecology, University of Maine; the Maine Agricultural and Forest Experiment Station; the National Park Service; and the U.S. Fish and Wildlife Service. 1994. Miscellaneous Publication 721. Available from: Publications Office, Room 1, Maine Agricultural and Forest Expt. Station, 5782 Winslow Hall, University of Maine, Orono, ME 04469-5782; (207) 581-1110.

174   *Wetlands in the Watersheds of the New York Water Supply System*. R.W. Tiner. 1997. 17 pp. color booklet. Limited copies through U.S. Fish and Wildlife Service. Available from: Laurie Machung, New York City Department of Environmental Protection, Watershed Office of Public Affairs, 71 Smith Avenue, Kingston, NY 12401; (845) 340-7524.

       Mid Atlantic Wetlands - A Disappearing Natural Treasure. R.W. Tiner, Jr., June 1987. http://library.fws.gov/Wetlands/midatlantic.pdf

       Wetlands of Saratoga County, New York. R. Tiner. 2000. 20 pp. color booklet. A Cooperative National Wetlands Inventory Report. http://www.fws.gov/wetlands/_documents/gOther/ WetlandsSaratogaCounty.pdf

Wetlands of Staten Island, New York. R. Tiner. 2000. 20 pp. color booklet. A Cooperative National Wetlands Inventory Report. http://www.fws.gov/wetlands/_documents/gOther/WetlandsStatenIsland.pdf

180   *Wetlands and Deepwater Habitats at Saratoga County, New York; The Results of the National Wetlands Inventory,* by R.W. Tiner, I.K. Huber, D.B. Foulis, T. Nuerminger, G.S. Smith and M. J. Starr. 2000.

Geographically Isolated Wetlands: A Preliminary Assessment of Their Characteristics and Status in Selected Areas of the United States 2002. U.S. Fish and Wildlife Service, Northeast Region, Hadley, MA. http://www.fws.gov/wetlands/_documents/gOther/GeographicallyIsolatedWetlandsFS.pdf

Wetlands of the Boston Harbor Islands National Recreation Area by R. W. Tiner, J. Q. Swords, and H.C. Bergquist. 2003. U.S. Fish and Wildlife Service, Northeast Region, Hadley, MA. http://library.fws.gov/wetlands/boston_harbor03.pdf.

SUBMERGED AQUATIC VEGETATION SURVEYS

Eelgrass Survey for Eastern Long Island Sound, Connecticut and New York. R. Tiner, H. Bergquist, T. Halavick, and A. MacLachlan. 2003.

2006 Eelgrass Survey for Eastern Long Island Sound, Connecticut and New York. R. Tiner, H. Bergquist, T. Halavick, and A. MacLachlan. 2007. http://library.fws.gov/Wetlands/eelgrass_report_2006.pdf

An Inventory of Submerged Aquatic Vegetation and Hardened Shorelines of the Peconic Estuary, New York by R.W. Tiner and others. 2003. http://library.fws.gov/Wetlands/peconic03.pdf

WETLAND RESTORATION AND CREATION (INCLUDING STREAM BUFFERS)

175   *Wetland Restoration and Creation* by R.W. Tiner. 1995.

Managing Common Reed (Phragmites australis) in Massachusetts: An Introduction to the Species and Control Techniques by R. Tiner. 1998. http//www.massaudubon.org/Kids/Lively_Lessons/Saltmarsh/restoration.html

187   *Restoring Wetland and Streamside/Riparian Buffers* by R.W. Tiner. 2003.

WETLAND MONITORING

179   *Wetland Monitoring Guidelines: Operational Draft.* U.S. Fish and Wildlife Service, Region 5, Hadley, MA.

WETLAND EVALUATION/ASSESSMENT

Correlating Enhanced National Wetlands Inventory Data with Wetland Functions for Watershed Assessments: A Rationale for Northeastern U.S. Wetlands by R. Tiner, October 2003. http://wetlands.fws.gov/Pubs_Reports/HGMReportOctober2003.pdf

WATERSHED-BASED WETLAND STUDIES: CHARACTERIZATION AND PRELIMINARY FUNCTIONAL ASSESSMENT, WETLAND RESTORATION, AND OVERALL ECOLOGICAL INTEGRITY

Historical Analysis of Wetlands and Their Functions for the Nanticoke River Watershed: A Comparison Between Pre-settlement and 1998 Conditions. R. W. Tiner and H.C. Bergquist. 2003. http://library.fws.gov/wetlands/Nanticoke04.pdf

An Inventory of Coastal Wetlands, Potential Restoration Sites, Wetland Buffers, and Hardened Shorelines for the Narragansett Bay Estuary: An Assessment Report from the National Wetlands Inventory Program. R.W. Tiner and others. 2003. http://library.fws.gov/wetlands/RIcoast03.pdf

The Parker River Watershed: An Assessment of Recent Trends in Salt Marshes, Their Buffers, and River-Stream Buffer Zones (1985-1999). 2002. http://library.fws.gov/wetlands/parkerriver02.pdf

Wetland Characterization and Preliminary Assessment of Wetland Functions for the Delaware and Catskill Watersheds of the New York City Water Supply System. R.W. Tiner and J. Stewart. 2004.

Wetland Characterization and Preliminary Assessment of Wetland Functions for the Croton Watershed of the New York City Water Supply System. R.W.Tiner, C.W. Polzen, and B. J. McClain. 2004.

Watershed-based Wetland Characterization for Maryland's Nanticoke River and Coastal Bays Watersheds: A Preliminary Assessment Report. R.W. Tiner and others. 2000. http://www.fws.gov/wetlands/_documents/gOther/WatershedbasedWetlandCharacterizationMarylandsNanticokeRiverWatershed.pdf

Watershed-based Wetland Characterizations for Delaware's Nanticoke River Watershed: A Preliminary Assessment Report. R.W. Tiner and others. 2001. http://library.fws.gov/wetlands/DEnanticoke01.pdf

197   *Enhancing Wetlands Inventory Data for Watershed-based Wetland Characterizations and Preliminary Assessments of Wetland Functions.* R.W. Tiner. 2002.

198   *Remotely-sensed Natural Habitat Integrity Indices for Assessing the General Ecological Condition of Watersheds.* R.W. Tiner. 2002

         Watershed-based Wetland Planning and Evaluation. A Collection of Papers from the Wetland Millennium Event (August 6-12, 2000; Quebec City, Quebec, Canada). http://www.aswm.org/propub/pubs/pdf/tiner_2002_wshed.pdf

180   *Wetland Characterization Study and Preliminary Assessment of Wetland Functions for the Casco Bay Watershed, Southern Maine.* by R.W. Tiner and others. 1999. U.S. Fish and Wildlife Service, Region 5, Hadley, MA.

185   *Wetland Characterization and Preliminary Assessment of Wetland Functions for the Boyds Corner and West Branch Sub-basins of the Croton Watershed, New York* by R. Tiner, S. Schaller, and M. Starr. 1999.

193   *Wetlands and Potential Wetland Restoration Sites for the Mill Rivers and Manhan River Watershed.* R.W. Tiner and others. 2000

194   *Wetlands and Potential Wetland Restoration Sites for the Shawsheen Watershed.* R.W. Tiner and others. 2000. (Cooperative USFWS and University of Massachusetts report)

         Correlating Enhanced National Wetlands Inventory Data with Wetland Functions for Watershed Assessments: A Rationale for Northeastern U.S. Wetlands by R. Tiner, October 2003. http://library.fws.gov/Wetlands/corelate_wetlandsNE.pdf

         Remotely-sensed indicators for monitoring the general condition of "natural habitat" in watersheds: an application for Delaware's Nanticoke River watershed by R. Tiner. Published in Ecological Indicators 4 (2004): 227-243. Contact ralph_tiner@fws.gov for copy.

205   Wetlands and Potential Wetland Restoration Sites for the Upper Ipswich Watershed.

WETLAND PROTECTION

201   *Geographically Isolated Wetlands of the United States* by R.W. Tiner, U. S. Fish and Wildlife Service. Wetlands, Vol 23, No.3, Sept. 2003, pp. 494-516, The Society of Wetland Scientists.

APPENDIX D. TABULUAR SUMMARIES OF NWI FINDINGS FOR EACH STATE AND THE DISTRICT OF COLUMBIA

(Note: Data are presented for each area alphabetically. Two tables are given: one for wetlands and the other for deepwater habitat totals.)

Connecticut

Table CT-1. Acreage of wetlands for Connecticut based on NWI data in the national database as of September 2009 (see Figure 5 for locations and effective date of data based on imagery).

System	Subsystem	Class	Acreage
Estuarine	Intertidal	Aquatic Bed	94
		Emergent	12,128
		Scrub-Shrub	57
		Rocky Shore	116
		Unconsolidated Shore	6,393
	Total Estuarine		**18,788**
Palustrine	--	Aquatic Bed	238
		Emergent	12,613 (1,225 = tidal)
		Forested	106,463 (50 = tidal)
		Scrub-Shrub	27,818 (349 = tidal)
		Farmed	1
		Unconsolidated Bottom	34,135 (45 = tidal)
		Unconsolidated Shore	18
	Total Palustrine		**181,286 (1,669 = tidal)**
Lacustrine	Littoral	Aquatic Bed	565
		Emergent	185
		Unconsolidated Bottom	741
		Unconsolidated Shore	22
	Total Lacustrine		**1,513**
Riverine	Tidal	Emergent	167
		Unconsolidated Shore	84
		(Subtotal)	(251)
	Lower Perennial	Rocky Shore	16
		Unconsolidated Shore	24
		(Subtotal)	(40)
	Upper Perennial	Unconsolidated Shore	1
	Total Riverine		**292**
TOTAL MAPPED			**201,879**

Table CT-2. Acreage of deepwater habitats for Connecticut based on NWI data in the national database as of September 2009 (see Figure 5 for locations and effective date of data based on imagery).

System	Subsystem	Class	Acreage
Estuarine	Subtidal	Unconsolidated Bottom (UB)	349, 005
	Total Estuarine		**349,005**
Lacustrine	Limnetic	Aquatic Bed (UB)	87
		Unconsolidated Bottom	36,254
	Total Lacustrine		**36,341**
Riverine	Tidal	Unconsolidated Bottom	7,356
	Lower Perennial	Rocky Shore	86
		Unconsolidated Bottom	4,819
		(Subtotal)	(4,905)
	Upper Perennial	Unconsolidated Bottom	2,422
	Total Riverine		**14,683**
TOTAL MAPPED			400,029

Delaware

Table DE-1. Acreage of wetlands for Delaware based on NWI data in the national database as of September 2009 (see Figure 5 for locations and effective date of data based on imagery).

System	Subsystem	Class	Acreage
Marine	Interidal	Unconsolidated Shore	622
	Total Marine		**622**
Estuarine	Intertidal	Emergent	77,256
		Forested	11
		Scrub-Shrub	935
		Unconsolidated Shore	4,880
	Total Estuarine		**83,082**
Palustrine	--	Aquatic Bed	14 (7 = tidal)
		Emergent	11,805 (3,229 = tidal)
		Forested	146,412 (5,520 = tidal)
		Scrub-Shrub	13,163 (1,550 = tidal)
		Farmed	3,370
		Unconsolidated Bottom	3,780 (562 = tidal)
		Unconsolidated Shore	341 (146 = tidal)
	Total Palustrine		**178,885 (11,014 = tidal)**
Lacustrine	Littoral	Emergent	12
		Unconsolidated Bottom	42
	Total Lacustrine		**54**
Riverine	Tidal	Emergent	239
		Unconsolidated Shore	195
	Total Riverine		**434**
TOTAL MAPPED			263,077

Table DE-2. Acreage of deepwater habitats for Delaware based on NWI data in the national database as of September 2009 (see Figure 5 for locations and effective date of data based on imagery).

System	Subsystem	Class	Acreage
Marine	Subtidal	Unconsolidated Bottom	54,873
	Total Marine		*54,873*
Estuarine	Subtidal	Unconsolidated Bottom	271,779
	Total Estuarine		271,779
Lacustrine	Limnetic	Unconsolidated Bottom	4,176
	Total Lacustrine		*4,176*
Riverine	Tidal	Unconsolidated Bottom	3,762
	Lower Perennial	Unconsolidated Bottom	487
	Total Riverine		*4,249*
TOTAL MAPPED			335,077

District of Columbia

Table DC-1. Acreage of wetlands and deepwater habitats for District of Columbia, DC based on NWI data in the national database as of September 2009 (see Figure 5 for locations and effective date of data based on imagery).

System	Subsystem	Class	Acreage
Palustrine	--	Aquatic Bed	9
		Emergent	12 (7 = tidal)
		Forested	183 (79 = tidal)
		Scrub-Shrub	9 (1 = tidal)
		Unconsolidated Bottom	23 (2 = tidal)
		Unconsolidated Shore	1
	Total Palustrine		*237 (89 = tidal)*
Lacustrine	Littoral	Emergent	26
		Unconsolidated Shore	1
	Total Lacustrine		*27*
Riverine	Tidal	Emergent	30
		Unconsolidated Shore	111
		(Subtotal)	(141)
	Lower Perennial	Unconsolidated Shore	4
	Upper Perennial	Unconsolidated Shore	4
	Total Riverine		*149*
TOTAL MAPPED			413

Table DC-2. Acreage of deepwater habitats for the District of Columbia based on NWI data in the national database as of September 2009 (see Figure 5 for locations and effective date of data based on imagery).

System	Subsystem	Class	Acreage
Lacustrine	Limnetic	Unconsolidated Bottom	319
	Total Lacustrine		*319*
Riverine	Tidal	Unconsolidated Bottom	3,928
	Upper Perennial	Unconsolidated Bottom	16
	Total Riverine		*3.944*
TOTAL MAPPED			4,263

Maine

Table ME-1. Acreage of wetlands for Maine based on NWI data in the national database as of September 2009 (see Figure 5 for locations and effective date of data based on imagery).

System	Subsystem	Class	Acreage
Marine	Interidal	Aquatic Bed	13,268
		Rocky Shore	30,141
		Unconsolidated Shore	26,407
	Total Marine		**69,816**
Estuarine	Intertidal	Aquatic Bed	6,853
		Emergent	22,539
		Scrub-Shrub	99
		Rocky Shore	2,058
		Streambed	6
		Unconsolidated Shore	51,620
	Total Estuarine		**83,175**
Palustrine	--	Aquatic Bed	139
		Emergent	200,952 (2,203 = tidal)
		Forested	1,194,848 (6,144 = tidal)
		Scrub-Shrub	547,999 (3,508 = tidal)
		Farmed	184
		Cultivated Cranberry Bog	307
		Unconsolidated Bottom	55,658 (403 = tidal)
		Unconsolidated Shore	806 (2 = tidal)
	Total Palustrine		**2,000,893 (12,260 = tidal)**
Lacustrine	Littoral	Aquatic Bed	115
		Emergent	260
		Rocky Shore	7,950
		Unconsolidated Bottom	458
		Unconsolidated Shore	7,712
	Total Lacustrine		**16,495**

Riverine	Tidal	Aquatic Bed	11
		Emergent	86
		Rocky Shore	3
		Unconsolidated Shore	2,320
		(Subtotal)	(2,420)
	Lower Perennial	Emergent	13
		Rocky Shore	38
		Unconsolidated Shore	1,185
		(Subtotal)	(1,236)
	Upper Perennial	Rocky Shore	13
		Unconsolidated Shore	1,083
		(Subtotal)	(1,096)
	Total Riverine		*4,753*
TOTAL MAPPED			**2,175,132**

Table ME-2. Acreage of deepwater habitats for Maine based on NWI data in the national database as of September 2009 (see Figure 5 for locations and effective date of data based on imagery).

System	Subsystem	Class	Acreage
Marine	Subtidal	Aquatic Bed	2,557
		Unconsolidated Bottom	1,343,315
	Total Marine		*1,345,872*
Estuarine	Subtidal	Aquatic Bed	12
		Rock Bottom	13
		Unconsolidated Bottom	78,922
	Total Estuarine		*78,937*
Lacustrine	Limnetic	Aquatic Bed	14
		Unconsolidated Bottom	922,782
	Total Lacustrine		*922,796*
Riverine	Tidal	Rock Bottom	3
		Unconsolidated Bottom	6,554
		(Subtotal)	(6,557)
	Lower Perennial	Rock Bottom	59
		Unconsolidated Bottom	69,659
		(Subtotal)	(69,718)
	Upper Perennial	Rock Bottom	122
		Unconsolidated Bottom	155,897
		(Subtotal)	(16,019)
	Total Riverine		*92,294*
TOTAL MAPPED			**2,439,899**

Maryland

Table MD-1. Acreage of wetlands for Maryland based on NWI data in the national database as of September 2009 (see Figure 5 for locations and effective date of data based on imagery).

System	Subsystem	Class	Acreage
Marine	Interidal	Unconsolidated Shore	722
	Total Marine		**722**
Estuarine	Intertidal	Emergent	205,184
		Forested	16,870
		Scrub-Shrub	2,488
		Rocky Shore	2
		Unconsolidated Shore	23,670
	Total Estuarine		**248,214**
Palustrine	--	Aquatic Bed	426
		Emergent	33,958 (3,955 = tidal)
		Forested	359,897 (36,960 = tidal)
		Scrub-Shrub	35,932 (2,926 = tidal)
		Farmed	662
		Rock Bottom	140
		Unconsolidated Bottom	16,649 (248 = tidal)
		Unconsolidated Shore	550 (2 = tidal)
	Total Palustrine		**448,214 (44,091 = tidal)**
Lacustrine	Littoral	Aquatic Bed	6
		Emergent	535
		Rocky Shore	8
		Unconsolidated Bottom	139
		Unconsolidated Shore	727
	Total Lacustrine		**1,415**

Riverine	Tidal	Emergent	1,574
		Unconsolidated Shore	176
		(Subtotal)	(1,750)
	Lower Perennial	Emergent	6
		Unconsolidated Shore	126
		(Subtotal)	(132)
	Upper Perennial	Rocky Shore	6
		Unconsolidated Shore	48
		(Subtotal)	(54)
	Unknown Perennial	Rocky Shore	4
		Unconsolidated Shore	11
		(Subtotal)	(15)
	Total Riverine		*1,951*
TOTAL MAPPED			**700,516**

Table MD-2. Acreage of deepwater habitats for Maryland based on NWI data in the national database as of September 2009 (see Figure 5 for locations and effective date of data based on imagery).

System	Subsystem	Class	Acreage
Marine	Subtidal	Unconsolidated Bottom	57,415
	Total Marine		*57,415*
Estuarine	Subtidal	Aquatic Bed	2
		Unconsolidated Bottom	1,541,508
	Total Estuarine		*1,541,510*
Lacustrine	Limnetic	Unconsolidated Bottom	20,956
	Total Lacustrine		*20,956*
Riverine	Tidal	Unconsolidated Bottom	17,100
	Lower Perennial	Unconsolidated Bottom	11,660
	Upper Perennial	Rock Bottom	373
		Unconsolidated Bottom	2,350
		(Subtotal)	(2,723)
	Unknown Perennial	Unconsolidated Bottom	7,150
	Total Riverine		*38,633*
TOTAL MAPPED			1,658,514

Massachusetts

Table MA-1. Acreage of wetlands for Massachusetts based on NWI data in the national database as of September 2009. For this state, the data reflect acreage statistics for 98% of the state where NWI digital data are available (see Figure 5 for locations and effective date of data based on imagery).

System	Subsystem	Class	Acreage
Marine	Interidal	Aquatic Bed	930
		Reef	26
		Rocky Shore	825
		Unconsolidated Shore	19,488
Total Marine			**21,269**
Estuarine	Intertidal	Aquatic Bed	254
		Emergent	44,894
		Forested	2
		Scrub-Shrub	1,009
		Reef	64
		Rocky Shore	130
		Unconsolidated Shore	15,501
Total Estuarine			**61,854**
Palustrine	--	Aquatic Bed	684
		Emergent	39,682 (1,182 = tidal)
		Forested	293,268 (1,808 = tidal)
		Scrub-Shrub	84,562 (1,483 = tidal)
		Farmed	55
		Cultivated Cranberry Bog	4,473
		Unconsolidated Bottom	26,983 (328 = tidal)
		Unconsolidated Shore	407 (24 = tidal)
Total Palustrine			**450,114 (4,825 = tidal)**
Lacustrine	Littoral	Aquatic Bed	1,303
		Emergent	1,104
		Unconsolidated Bottom	432
		Unconsolidated Shore	135
Total Lacustrine			**2,974**

Riverine	Tidal	Emergent	6
	Lower Perennial	Rocky Shore	7
		Unconsolidated Shore	65
		(Subtotal)	(72)
	Upper Perennial	Unconsolidated Shore	21
	Unknown Perennial	Unconsolidated Shore	1
	Intermittent	Unconsolidated Shore	68
	Total Riverine		*168*
TOTAL MAPPED			536,379

Table MA-2. Acreage of deepwater habitats for Massachusetts based on NWI data in the national database as of September 2009. For this state, the data reflect acreage statistics for 98% of the state where NWI digital data are available (see Figure 5 for locations and effective date of data based on imagery).

System	Subsystem	Class	Acreage
Marine	Subtidal	Aquatic Bed	24,767
		Unconsolidated Bottom	1,024,125
	Total Marine		*1,048,892*
Estuarine	Subtidal	Aquatic Bed	7,624
		Unconsolidated Bottom	89,835
	Total Estuarine		*97,459*
Lacustrine	Limnetic	Aquatic Bed (AB)	45
		Unconsolidated Bottom	124,311
		Unconsolidated Bottom/AB	122
	Total Lacustrine		*124,478*
Riverine	Tidal	Unconsolidated Bottom	951
	Lower Perennial	Rock Bottom	7
		Unconsolidated Bottom	17,244
		(Subtotal)	(17,251)
	Upper Perennial	Unconsolidated Bottom	2,253
	Unknown Perennial	Unconsolidated Bottom	1,109
	Total Riverine		*21,564*
TOTAL MAPPED			1,292,393

New Hampshire

Table NH-1. Acreage of wetlands for New Hampshire based on NWI data in the national database as of September 2009 (see Figure 5 for locations and effective date of data based on imagery).

System	Subsystem	Class	Acreage
Marine	Interidal	Aquatic Bed	225
		Rocky Shore	161
		Unconsolidated Shore	500
	Total Marine		**886**
Estuarine	Intertidal	Aquatic Bed	106
		Emergent	5,904
		Scrub-Shrub	7
		Rocky Shore	7
		Unconsolidated Shore	3,273
	Total Estuarine		**9,297**
Palustrine	--	Aquatic Bed	199
		Emergent	39,452 (110 = tidal)
		Forested	140,451 (520 = tidal)
		Scrub-Shrub	73,984 (164 = tidal)
		Farmed	1
		Unconsolidated Bottom	26,101 (60 = tidal)
		Unconsolidated Shore	46
	Total Palustrine		**280,234 (854 = tidal)**
Lacustrine	Littoral	Aquatic Bed	85
		Emergent	122
		Unconsolidated Bottom	190
		Unconsolidated Shore	301
	Total Lacustrine		**698**
Riverine	Lower Perennial	Unconsolidated Shore	713
	Upper Perennial	Rocky Shore	6
		Unconsolidated Shore	701
		(Subtotal)	(707)
	Unknown Perennial	Unconsolidated Shore	1
	Intermittent	Unconsolidated Shore	34
	Total Riverine		**1,455**
TOTAL MAPPED			292,570

Table NH-2. Acreage of deepwater habitats for New Hampshire based on NWI data in the national database as of September 2009 (see Figure 5 for locations and effective date of data based on imagery).

System	Subsystem	Class	Acreage
Marine	Subtidal	Unconsolidated Bottom	42,842
	Total Marine		*42,842*
Estuarine	Subtidal	Unconsolidated Bottom (UB)	7,659
		Aquatic Bed/UB	52
	Total Estuarine		*7,711*
Lacustrine	Limnetic	Unconsolidated Bottom	166,859
	Total Lacustrine		*124,478*
Riverine	Tidal	Unconsolidated Bottom	27
	Lower Perennial	Unconsolidated Bottom	17,867
	Upper Perennial	Unconsolidated Bottom	1,782
	Unknown Perennial	Unconsolidated Bottom	1
	Total Riverine		*19,677*
TOTAL MAPPED			237,089

New Jersey

Table NJ-1. Acreage of wetlands for New Jersey based on NWI data in the national database as of September 2009 (see Figure 5 for locations and effective date of data based on imagery).

System	Subsystem	Class	Acreage
Marine	Interidal	Rocky Shore	12
		Unconsolidated Shore	4,212
	Total Marine		**4,224**
Estuarine	Intertidal	Aquatic Bed	40
		Emergent	201,837
		Forested	77
		Scrub-Shrub	1,603
		Rocky Shore	2
		Unconsolidated Shore	5,154
	Total Estuarine		**208,713**
Palustrine	--	Aquatic Bed	131 (17 = tidal)
		Emergent	67,314 (10,557 = tidal)
		Forested	515,951 (18,870 = tidal)
		Scrub-Shrub	102,610 (10,584 = tidal)
		Farmed	2,811
		Cultivated Cranberry Bog	4,500
		Unconsolidated Bottom	25,782 (757 = tidal)
		Unconsolidated Shore	802 (116 = tidal)
	Total Palustrine		**719,991 (40,901 = tidal)**
Lacustrine	Littoral	Rock Bottom	34
		Unconsolidated Bottom	580
		Unconsolidated Shore	170
	Total Lacustrine		**784**
Riverine	Tidal	Emergent	660
		Unconsolidated Shore	2,071
		(Subototal)	(2,731)
	Lower Perennial	Emergent	57
		Unconsolidated Shore	49
		(Subtotal)	(106)
	Intermittent	Streambed	154
		Unconsolidated Shore	283
		(Subtotal)	(437)
	Total Riverine		**3,274**
TOTAL MAPPED			936,986

Table NJ-2. Acreage of deepwater habitats for New Jersey based on NWI data in the national database as of September 2009 (see Figure 5 for locations and effective date of data based on imagery).

System	Subsystem	Class	Acreage
Marine	Subtidal	Unconsolidated Bottom	308,601
	Total Marine		*308,601*
Estuarine	Subtidal	Unconsolidated Bottom	508,179
	Total Estuarine		*508,179*
Lacustrine	Limnetic	Unconsolidated Bottom	50,594
	Total Lacustrine		*50,594*
Riverine	Tidal	Unconsolidated Bottom	13,525
	Lower Perennial	Unconsolidated Bottom	12,371
	Upper Perennial	Rock Bottom Unconsolidated Bottom	8 766 (774)
	Total Riverine		*26,670*
TOTAL MAPPED			894,044

New York

Table NY-1. Acreage of wetlands for New York based on NWI data in the national database as of September 2009. For this state, the data reflect acreage statistics for 74% of the state where NWI digital data are available (see Figure 5 for locations and effective date of data based on imagery).

System	Subsystem	Class	Acreage
Marine	Interidal	Aquatic Bed	8
		Rocky Shore	18
		Unconsolidated Shore	4,957
	Total Marine		*4,983*
Estuarine	Intertidal	Aquatic Bed	249
		Emergent	27,684
		Forested	8
		Scrub-Shrub	1,077
		Rocky Shore	69
		Unconsolidated Shore	7,074
	Total Estuarine		*36,161*
Palustrine	--	Aquatic Bed	1,208 (1 = tidal)
		Emergent	219,944 (1,558 = tidal)
		Forested	892,019 (2,570 = tidal)
		Scrub-Shrub	257,411 (499 = tidal)
		Farmed	21,731
		Unconsolidated Bottom	92,773 (229 = tidal)
		Unconsolidated Shore	760
	Total Palustrine		*1,485,846 (4,857 = tidal)*
Lacustrine	Littoral	Aquatic Bed	2,051
		Emergent	694
		Rocky Shore	48
		Unconsolidated Bottom	33,553
		Unconsolidated Shore	3,291
	Total Lacustrine		*39,637*

Riverine	Tidal	Aquatic Bed	4
		Emergent	9
		Unconsolidated Shore	427
		(Subotatol)	(440)
	Lower Perennial	Aquatic Bed	1,151
		Emergent	164
		Rocky Shore	15
		Unconsolidated Shore	1,593
		(Subtotal)	(2,923)
	Upper Perennial	Unconsolidated Shore	1,658
	Unknown Perennial	Emergent	71
		Rocky Shore	11
		Unconsolidated Shore	72
		(Subtotal)	(154)
	Intermittent	Streambed	38
		Unconsolidated Shore	913
		(Subtotal)	(951)
	Total Riverine		*6,126*
TOTAL MAPPED			**1,572,753**

Table NY-2. Acreage of deepwater habitats for New York based on NWI data in the national database as of September 2009. For this state, the data reflect acreage statistics for 74% of the state where NWI digital data are available (see Figure 5 for locations and effective date of data based on imagery).

System	Subsystem	Class	Acreage
Marine	Subtidal	Aquatic Bed	1,501
		Unconsolidated Bottom	784,398
	Total Marine		*785,899*
Estuarine	Subtidal	Aquatic Bed	28,374
		Unconsolidated Bottom	818,864
	Total Estuarine		*847,238*
Lacustrine	Limnetic	Aquatic Bed	152
		Unconsolidated Bottom	1,174,429
	Total Lacustrine		*1,174,581*
Riverine	Tidal	Unconsolidated Bottom	25,425
	Lower Perennial	Rock Bottom	3
		Unconsolidated Bottom	105,090
		(Subtotal)	(105,093)
	Upper Perennial	Rock Bottom	441
		Unconsolidated Bottom	12,203
		(Subtotal)	(13,644)
	Unknown Perennial	Unconsolidted Bottom	1,065
	Total Riverine		*145,227*
TOTAL MAPPED			2,952,945

Pennsylvania

Table PA-1. Acreage of wetlands for Pennsylvania based on NWI data in the national database as of September 2009 (see Figure 5 for locations and effective date of data based on imagery).

System	Subsystem	Class	Acreage
Estuarine	Intertidal	Unconsolidated Shore	55
	Total Estuarine		*55*
Palustrine	--	Aquatic Bed	1,314
		Emergent	59,023 (200 = tidal)
		Forested	219,101 (220 = tidal)
		Scrub-Shrub	79,589 (13 = tidal)
		Farmed	2
		Rock Bottom	92
		Unconsolidated Bottom	60,452 (5 =tidal)
		Unconsolidated Shore	545 (41 = tidal)
	Total Palustrine		*420,118 (479 = tidal)*
Lacustrine	Littoral	Aquatic Bed	892
		Emergent	266
		Rock Bottom	95
		Rocky Shore	120
		Unconsolidated Bottom	6,215
		Unconsolidated Shore	1,221
	Total Lacustrine		*8,809*
Riverine	Tidal	Emergent	157
		Unconsolidated Shore	760
		(Subtotal)	(917)
	Lower Perennial	Emergent	517
		Rocky Shore	31
		Unconsolidated Shore	1,088
		(Subtotal)	(1,636)
	Upper Perennial	Rocky Shore	67
		Unconsolidated Shore	434
		(Subtotal)	(501)
	Unknown Perennial	Emergent	88
		Unconsolidated Shore	248
		(Subtotal)	(336)
	Intermittent	Unconsolidated Shore	275
	Total Riverine		*3,665*
TOTAL WETLANDS			432,647

61

Table PA-2. Acreage of deepwater habitats for Pennsylvania based on NWI data in the national database as of September 2009 (see Figure 5 for locations and effective date of data based on imagery).

System	Subsystem	Class	Acreage
Estuarine	Subtidal	Unconsolidated Bottom (UB)	647
	Total Estuarine		*647*
Lacustrine	Limnetic	Aquatic Bed (UB)	69
		Unconsolidated Bottom (UB)	312,140
	Total Lacustrine		*312,209*
Riverine	Tidal	Unconsolidated Bottom	9,478
	Lower Perennial	Rock Bottom	92
		Unconsolidated Bottom	139,232
		(Subtotal)	(139,324)
	Upper Perennial	Rock Bottom	46
		Unconsolidated Bottom	13,462
		(Subtotal)	(13,508)
	Unknown Perennial	Unconsolidated Bottom	8,421
	Total Riverine		*170,731*
TOTAL MAPPED			483,587

Rhode Island

Table RI-1. Acreage of wetlands for Rhode Island based on NWI data in the national database as of September 2009 (see Figure 5 for locations and effective date of data based on imagery).

System	Subsystem	Class	Acreage
Marine	Interidal	Aquatic Bed	1
		Rocky Shore	215
		Unconsolidated Shore	714
	Total Marine		***930***
Estuarine	Intertidal	Aquatic Bed	42
		Emergent	3,678
		Forested	80
		Scrub-Shrub	3
		Rocky Shore	62
		Streambed	4
		Unconsolidated Shore	3,419
	Total Estuarine		***7,288***
Palustrine	--	Aquatic Bed	37
		Emergent	3,051 (34 = tidal)
		Forested	48,665 (94 = tidal)
		Scrub-Shrub	5,887 (16 = tidal)
		Cultivated Cranberry Bog	107
		Unconsolidated Bottom	4,680 (25 = tidal)
		Unconsolidated Shore	27 (8 = tidal)
	Total Palustrine		***62,454 (177 = tidal)***
Lacustrine	Littoral	Emergent	4
		Unconsolidated Shore	2
	Total Lacustrine		***6***
TOTAL WETLANDS			70,678

Table RI-2. Acreage of deepwater habitats for Rhode Island based on NWI data in the national database as of September 2009 (see Figure 5 for locations and effective date of data based on imagery).

System	Subsystem	Class	Acreage
Marine	Subtidal	Aquatic Bed	1,175
		Unconsolidated Bottom	171,455
	Total Marine		*172,630*
Estuarine	Subtidal	Aquatic Bed	357
		Unconsolidated Bottom	88,033
	Total Estuarine		*88,390*
Lacustrine	Limnetic	Unconsolidated Bottom	19,484
	Total Lacustrine		*19,484*
Riverine	Tidal	Unconsolidated Bottom	20
	Lower Perennial	Unconsolidated Bottom	1,059
	Total Riverine		*1,079*
TOTAL MAPPED			281,583

Vermont

Table VT-1. Acreage of wetlands for Vermont based on NWI data in the national database as of September 2009. For this state, the data reflect acreage statistics for 99% of the state where NWI digital data are available (see Figure 5 for locations and effective date of data based on imagery).

System	Subsystem	Class	Acreage
Palustrine	--	Aquatic Bed	583
		Emergent	47,222
		Forested	117,801
		Scrub-Shrub	59,947
		Farmed	1,114
		Unconsolidated Bottom	13,717
		Unconsolidated Shore	80
	Total Palustrine		*240,464*
Lacustrine	Littoral	Aquatic Bed	1,188
		Emergent	28
		Unconsolidated Bottom	21,129
		Unconsolidated Shore	92
	Total Lacustrine		*22,437*
Riverine	Lower Perennial	Unconsolidated Shore	242
	Upper Perennial	Rocky Shore	2
		Unconsolidated Shore	193
		(Subtotal)	(195)
	Intermittent	Unconsolidated Shore	45
	Total Riverine		*482*
TOTAL MAPPED			263,383

Table VT-2. Acreage of deepwater habitats for Vermont based on NWI data in the national database as of September 2009. For this state, the data reflect acreage statistics for 99% of the state where NWI digital data are available (see Figure 5 for locations and effective date of data based on imagery).

System	Subsystem	Class	Acreage
Lacustrine	Limnetic	Aquatic Bed (AB)	19
		AB/Unconsolidated Bottom	2,516
		Unconsolidated Bottom (UB)	196,871
		UB/Aquatic Bed	20
	Total Lacustrine		*199,426*
Riverine	Lower Perennial	Rock Bottom	6
		Unconsolidated Bottom	10,698
		(Subtotal)	(10,704)
	Upper Perennial	Rock Bottom	171
		Unconsolidated Bottom	2,466
		(Subtotal)	(2,637)
	Total Riverine		*13,341*
TOTAL MAPPED			212,767

Virginia

Table VA-1. Acreage of wetlands for Virginia based on NWI data in the national database as of September 2009 (see Figure 5 for locations and effective date of data based on imagery).

System	Subsystem	Class	Acreage
Marine	Interidal	Aquatic Bed	37
		Reef	55
		Unconsolidated Shore	4,285
	Total Marine		*4,377*
Estuarine	Intertidal	Aquatic Bed	724
		Emergent	197,335
		Forested	3,670
		Scrub-Shrub	3,961
		Reef	705
		Rocky Shore	5
		Unconsolidated Shore	143,789
	Total Estuarine		*350,189*
Palustrine	--	Aquatic Bed	644 (23 = tidal)
		Emergent	107,743 (21,839 = tidal)
		Forested	811,100 (56,238 = tidal)
		Scrub-Shrub	103,902 (8,123 = tidal)
		Farmed	1,171
		Unconsolidated Bottom	82,291 (738 = tidal)
		Unconsolidated Shore	1,164 (10 = tidal)
	Total Palustrine		*1,108,015 (86,971 = tidal)*
Lacustrine	Littoral	Aquatic Bed	118
		Emergent	198
		Unconsolidated Bottom	3
		Unconsolidated Shore	1,462
			2,612
	Total Lacustrine		*4,393*

Riverine	Tidal	Emergent	500
		Unconsolidated Shore	2,047
		(Subtotal)	(2,547)
	Lower Perennial	Aquatic Bed	8
		Rocky Shore	11
		Unconsolidated Shore	420
		(Subtotal)	(439)
	Upper Perennial	Rocky Shore	18
		Unconsolidated Shore	215
		(Subtotal)	(233)
	Unknown Perennial	Emergent	2
		Rocky Shore	5
		Unconsolidated Shore	353
		(Subtotal)	(360)
	Intermittent	Streambed	2
		Unconsolidated Shore	157
		(Subtotal)	(159)
	Total Riverine		*3,738*
TOTAL MAPPED			1,470,712

Table VA-2. Acreage of deepwater habitats for Virginia based on NWI data in the national database as of September 2009 (see Figure 5 for locations and effective date of data based on imagery).

System	Subsystem	Class	Acreage
Marine	Subtidal	Unconsolidated Bottom	258,673
	Total Marine		**258,673**
Estuarine	Subtidal	Aquatic Bed	114
		Unconsolidated Bottom	1,361,893
	Total Estuarine		**1,362,007**
Lacustrine	Limnetic	Aquatic Bed	13
		Unconsolidated Bottom	139,656
	Total Lacustrine		**139,669**
Riverine	Tidal	Rock Bottom	5
		Unconsolidated Bottom	82,573
		(Subtotal)	(82,578)
	Lower Perennial	Rock Bottom	1
		Unconsolidated Bottom	51,064
		(Subtotal)	(51,065)
	Upper Perennial	Rock Bottom	62
		Unconsolidated Bottom	2,796
		(Subtotal)	(2,858)
	Unknown Perennial	Unconsolidted Bottom	10,235
	Total Riverine		**146,736**
TOTAL MAPPED			1,907,085

West Virginia

Table WV-1. Acreage of wetlands for West Virginia based on NWI data in the national database as of September 2009 (see Figure 5 for locations and effective date of data based on imagery).

System	Subsystem	Class	Acreage
Palustrine	--	Aquatic Bed	87
		Emergent	13,623
		Forested	12,762
		Scrub-Shrub	11,198
		Rock Bottom	29
		Unconsolidated Bottom	16,486
		Unconsolidated Shore	221
	Total Palustrine		*54,406*
Lacustrine	Littoral	Emergent	8
		Unconsolidated Bottom	30
		Unconsolidated Shore	2,512
	Total Lacustrine		*2,550*
Riverine	Lower Perennial	Emergent	6
		Unconsolidated Shore	385
		(Subtotal)	(391)
	Upper Perennial	Rocky Shore	226
		Unconsolidated Shore	384
		(Subtotal)	(610)
	Intermittent	Unconsolidated Shore	13
	Total Riverine		*1,442*
TOTAL MAPPED			58,398

Table WV-2. Acreage of deepwater habitats for West Virginia based on NWI data in the national database as of September 2009 (see Figure 5 for locations and effective date of data based on imagery).

System	Subsystem	Class	Acreage
Lacustrine	Limnetic	Unconsolidated Bottom	17,089
	Total Lacustrine		*17,089*
Riverine	Lower Perennial	Rock Bottom Unconsolidated Bottom (Subtotal)	11 54,270 (54,281)
	Upper Perennial	Rock Bottom Unconsolidated Bottom (Subtotal)	1,623 6,783 (8,406)
	Unknown Perennial	Rock Bottom Unconsolidated Bottom (Subtotal)	584 27,741 (28,325)
	Total Riverine		*91,012*
TOTAL MAPPED			108,101

U.S. Fish & Wildlife Service
http://www.fws.gov

April 2010

Cover photograph by Ralph Tiner, USFWS